DALITS IN ACTION

About the Author

Prof. A.K. Lal is a well known sociologist from Bihar having three decades of experience in research and training. Prof. Lal has worked on different themes and has successfully completed projects funded by the Central Government as well as Voluntary Organizations. He has special interests in the problems of dalits which finds articulation in his contributions facilitating understanding of the phenomenon of change and continuity among these people. He has long experience of field work in Bihar, Haryana, Madhya Pradesh and Delhi. Prof. Lal has been in close rapport with Sociological activities of the Sulabh International and has been founder Director of its institutions for research and social intervention. During his stay in the Sulabh International he organised courses for sanitation and rural development and helped the organization in initiating programmes for upliftment and social integration of scavengers. Prof. Lal has authored a number of books including the well known work on bonded labours in Bihar entitled *Politics of Poverty*. His other books are *The Urban Family, Elite and Development* (with Sachchidananda) and *Harijan Elite* (with Sachchidananda). His forthcoming books are *Secularism-Concept and Practice* and *Drug Abuse in Bihar*. In addition to these he has written a number of research articles and book reviews. Prof. Lal is presently a Senior Fellow (Sociology), G.B. Pant Social Science Institute, Allahabad.

DALITS IN ACTION
An Evaluation of Bihar Dalit Vikas Samiti

Prof. A.K. LAL
G.B. Pant Social Science Institute
Allahabad

CONCEPT PUBLISHING COMPANY, NEW DELHI - 110059

ISBN 81-7022-604-X

First Published 1997

Published and Printed by
Ashok Kumar Mittal
Concept Publishing Company
A/15-16, Commercial Block, Mohan Garden,
NEW DELHI - 110059 (India)
Phones : 5554042, 5504042

Foreword

India has made impressive achievements in the field of economic growth and social change. It seems poised to accelerate the process of attainment of prosperity with social equality. In fact this constitutes the fundamental intent of our national policies. The task is tremendous requiring involvement of different forces wedded to this goal. While economic development is difficult to attain, social change is still more difficult as it requires sustained efforts to erase the undesired evils of tradition. The State finds it difficult to remove inequality and exploitation legitimised through time immemorial. Its schemes for removal of exploitation of the poor and weak are not allowed to percolate down at the grass-root in the manner these are intended. The lowest among the low does not find himself empowered to question effectively the perpetuation of the status quo. Bondage and inertia keep them in the morass of degradation. Efforts are therefore, needed to take them out from a situation of helplessness. The Bihar Dalit Vikas Samiti represents one such initiative. The organization has tirelessly worked to see that dalits become self-reliant and rise against injustice. The present book takes a close look at the organization and functioning of the Samiti.

The author, Prof. A.K. Lal, Senior Fellow, Gobind Ballabh Pant Social Science Institute, Allahabad is a scholar of eminence. He has made distinctive contributions in the field of the study of the sociology of weaker sections. He has evinced sustained interest in this theme of immense social importance. While his early works on Dalits in India are well known and have been widely appreciated the present one represents his latest endeavour to provide understanding of a dimension that remained thoroughly neglected.

Prof. A.K. Lal has gone beyond the mandate of an evaluator. And it is a welcome departure. He has taken a critical look at the social, economic, political and cultural scenario in the villages of this northern state. His work does portray caste-based actions and interactions in the villages and the manner in which the people at the lowest rung of the society are maltreated.

The work in hand is a micro-study. It is addressed to rural

areas in a northern state. Yet its substantive concerns transcend regional boundaries. Perhaps information presented in the book has a wider validity. As such the work is bound to be of great interest to all those who look for a new perspective at the social scene on the subcontinent.

Bindeshwar Pathak

Preface

Dalits tend to represent the lowest among the lowly in the society. Their exploitation has been a legend. The various attributes of status congrue to accord them a highly disadvantaged location in social hierarchy. They are subjected to status disabilities. Their integration with the larger society remains an aspiration. Dalits seem to have been ignored in the schemes of economic development and social change. Power remains elusive in their case. Political modernisation also seems to have failed to lift them from a state of inertia. There is an urgent need to take them out from a situation of passivity so that they may assert for their due in the society. This is a difficult task as it involves bottom-up revolution. The present study tries to analyse the initiatives of a private sector enterprise towards empowerment of dalits.

I am obliged to Dr. Jose Kananaikil, Director, Bihar Dalit Vikas Samiti for inspiring me to take up the study and for providing the needed financial support to conduct it. The members of my research team deserve special thanks for their excellent field work. Shri Dipak Kumar Sinha and Shri Sudhir Kumar contributed immensely in the conduct of the project. Mr. M.J. Philip and Ms. Poonama George typed the manuscript. I am appreciative of their contributions. The title of this book has been suggested by my lovely little daughter Samriddhi, who is still a school student. I received help from my elder daughter Suprabha in drafting the report. The volume is dedicated to my mother Shrimati Bhagwati Devi, who used to tell me stories of atrocities on dalits while I was a child. Dr. Bindeshwar Pathak has been kind enough to write a foreword. His concern for the neglected and uncared has impressed me. I am obliged to him for his words of encouragement.

I am thankful to Sri Ashok Kumar Mittal of the Concept Publishing Company and members of his family for their support and encouragement.

A.K. Lal
G.B. Pant Social Science Institute
Allahabad (U.P.)

Contents

Contents

1

Introduction

I

Post-independent India has been witness to impressive achievements in the field of agriculture, industry, health, medical care and education. It has made significant strides in evolving a viable, productive infrastructure leading to substantive growth of national income. In spite of this, India remains one of the poorest countries of the world. Quality of life remains unchanged for the majority of the people. Power tends to be confined at the apex of the social hierarchy. Landholding and consumption statistics lend corroboration to the existence of discrimination against the bottom of the social hierarchy. India tends to remain a hierarchical and exploitative social order. Inequities in its worst form survives and poverty remains entrenched. Macro-indicators of development in fact seem to hide the realities at the grassroots. Failure of the redistributive intervention has placed India in a situation of deep troubles.

"The review of policies which were meant to achieve economic development within the broad objectives of a socialistic pattern of society" shows that whatever might have been the intentions, in reality policy measures have substantially gone to the benefit of the richer and more influential sections of society. Such categories as have inferior social-structural location have been unable to take advantage of their strength of number and remain 'written off ' by development. Modern development has left them impoverished and starving. It has deprived them of their due share forcing them to constitute the periphery in a situation of polarized power relations.

II

The failure of the state to ensure effective development has contributed significantly towards the proliferation of voluntary organisations wedded to the task of radical social transformation. These seem to have emerged as a result of the "disillusionment with the macro-level top-down managerial strategies of the government and partly as an historical outgrowth of indigenous traditions of services and voluntarism".[1] The voluntary sector signifies the impulse to renovate both the civil society and state in a situation characterised by disillusionment with the ineffective response of the state towards the sad plight of the large number of the people. "In sum, the grassroot initiatives in India today are in the nature of both a critique and protest against the prevailing model of development and the emergence of a new and alternative approach to rural development that is more holistic, that transcends economics and managerial ethics, in self-consciously political" and is political on behalf of the wretched on the earth.[2] Poor standards of bureaucratic performance and political in sincerity, insensitivity of the planning and delivery system constitute a source of inspiration and strength to such activism. In a situation characterised by development crisis, it has the capacity to activate mediating network to cushion "the isolated individual from the alienating bureaucracies and protects dissenting minorities from the tyranny of the majority and the powerful".[3] Thus the voluntary sector signifies the impulse to renovate the civil society and the state. It reflects a resurgence of counter-ideologies based on local, cultural, historical and indigenous factors. In a society ruled by "rootless elites" such organisations provide the basis for initiation of sincere and effective development process. These have to be seen "as typically oriented to the service of the victims of the state and civil society, the principal goal being existential amelioration of the victim groups".[4]

The context of increasing marginalisation of the poor and ineffectiveness of the state requires their presence. "In part they are performing new roles that have emerged in the new context of the human condition: a condition of profound marginalisation of millions of people and the social and moral vacuum created by the indifference of the system to it".[5]

These new missionaries mark the revival of community development programme of India in a new form where "development emphasises the expressed needs of the majority and aims at self-help and self-reliance of the community which can gainfully be attained by a decentralized, local, decision-making process".[6] Such infrastructures have to acquire a sustained existence in a milieu characterised by insensitivity of the state towards the worsening plight of the disadvantaged. The rise of this "non-party political process has to be seen not as transient happenings answering to contingent situations (or ad hoc expressions of some intriguing behaviour on the part of a few romantics) but rather as a historical phenomenon playing a specific social role and occupying a specific political space".[7]

III

The Bihar Dalit Vikas Samiti — an action programme originally initiated by the Indian Social Institute, New Delhi, is a non-political voluntary organization wedded to the task of uplift of the downtrodden. It is an important organization in the country engaged in social awareness, economic uplift and political consciousness among the neglected sections of the population. Its activities represent fresh initiatives in a sector that remained uncared demanding immediate attention. Among its target groups are scheduled castes and middle range caste men and women and other socio-cultural categories afflicted by poverty and subjected to exploitation. It is operative on behalf of those sections of society whom modern development has rendered impoverished, destitute and starving. As an organizational initiative it is poised to make development relevant to such sections of society which have "either been untouchables of development or when touched are affected adversely and became its victims". The intention is to effect social and political transformation of far-reaching consequences with long term implications.

Spread of social consciousness and organizations of the inert, dispersed masses seem to constitute its priority concern. Collective empowerment of the "dalits" in order to enable them to struggle for their due through aggregation of limited resources at their disposal is its primary objective. It intends to enable the marginalised group to federate themselves to seek redressal of the rights denied to them. Awareness of the situation confronting the dalits so as to prepare them to strive for implementation of their rights has to be ensured through social mobilization. The Samiti is oriented to make people conscious of their power through providing them an organization, and education. So far as it attempts at challenging the exploitative social order through federating the dalits for concerted group action, it represents a comprehensive measure for intervention in the historical process. It is poised to wage sustained struggle against the infrastructure of exploitation and oppression. It aims at induction of large section of the people relegated at the periphery to centre state in power structure. It intends to raise the consciousness among the inert sections of society to enable them to assert their rightful place in society. Vulnerable groups are organised to put united opposition against attempts to exploit them.

It has a distinctive approach to mobilize depressed sections of society around issues that are of concern to them. As such, it is a new social and political force intended to ensure people's participation to secure power and participation. It is a participatory organization of the rural poor emphasising local initiatives. It seeks alteration in socio-economic order through people's power.

Being empathetic to the needs and aspirations of the poor and disadvantaged, it emerges as an institutional framework to arrange succour for those in need. It operates in distant, uncared, politically dispossessed and economically distressed inhabitants in the remote rural areas and neglected urban centres. Included within the ambit of its objectives are issues and arenas of human activities that have been accorded scanty attention. In fulfilment of its tasks, it also intends to take up activities that otherwise should be the concern of the state. Thus, it also seeks to operate as an effective point in the delivery of basic inputs to neglected areas and disadvantaged people. Some of the tasks performed by it would have been in principle the duties of the extension agent under the community development programme. It seeks to make the people agents to their own development and change in their society. As an institutional network of support to the disadvantaged, it has often to step in the government shoes to operate as an important supplement to its delivery system.

The following constitute the detailed objectives of the Samiti:-

(a) To work for the integrated development of the oppressed all over India.

(b) To end untouchability in all its forms.

(c) To enable the oppressed to avail of governmental facilities for their social, economic and educational development and to awaken their political consciousness.

(d) To create classless, oppression-free villages based on non-violence and brotherhood.

(e) To mobilise people against injustice and exploitation and to ensure the oppressed justice and protection.

(f) To nurture unity, comradeship and co-operation amongst the oppressed.
(g) To remove all forms of diffidence and feeling of low status among the oppressed and to redeem their confidence and prestige.
(h) To raise voice against all forms of injustices and discrimination based on religion, caste and community.
(i) To ensure rights of allotment of land to the landless.
(j) To work for the freedom of bonded labourers and to ensure just wages for all.
(k) To improve living conditions of the poor with respect to hygiene, drainage, water, electricity, roads, houses, etc.
(l) To try to avail governmental facilities for the educated unemployed and to set up cottage and village industries and to conduct training programmes in tailoring, electronics, computer, etc.
(m) To encourage adult education, health, khadi industries and agricultural development and to discourage drinking and other social evils.
(n) To inspire women, children, the handicapped and other neglected and weaker groups in the path of progress.
(o) To do such work as shall help in achieving the Samiti's aims/goals.
(p) To collect necessary funds and to take up necessary or supplementary projects towards the fulfilment of the Samiti's aims/goals.

In sum the Bihar Dalit Vikas Samiti is a non-political voluntary organisation wedded to the task of uplift of the down-trodden. It seeks to create situations for concerted and consolidated action. It is oriented to fresh initiatives for the benefit of neglected and distressed sections of society. It represents a moderate non-violent activism based on the critique of power and domination and seeks in the ultimate to generate a countervailing power in the people. It is bottom-up initiative engaged in grassroot activities in contrast to the prevalent top-down approach for the amelioration of the exploited.

Objectives of the Study

The present study is an attempt to evaluate the working of the Bihar

Dalit Vikas Samiti — a community action group devoted to arousal of corporate striving among the dalits through constructive and people-oriented activism. It has been our endeavour to study the origin, growth and present status of this organisation. While analysing the activities of the organisation, we also intend to study the impact of its strategy for social transformation among the target groups concerned. Its achievements as well as limitations are to be documented to highlight the issues confronting this organisation devoted to the goal of ensuring social justice and citizenship privileges and participation to the deprived. The status characteristics of its core pattern of leadership and support, recruitment, strategies to usher in needed intervention constitute other parts of the enquiry. We have documented experiences in conducting different programmes to accomplish the objectives. Attempts have also been made to discern the extent of self-dependence and professionalism generated among the activists so as to make the movement sustainable.

The following are the detailed objectives of the study:-

(i) To document the history growth and of the organisation and elaborate its present activities.
(ii) To identify its agenda for social transformation.
(iii) To locate the issues that are of concern to the organisation and to elaborate the thrust of its activities.
(iv) To spell out the ideological terms in which its thinking on alternative approach for development is couched.
(v) To discuss the strategies activated for the attainment of the priorities.
(vi) To elaborate its organisational structure and style of work.
(vii) To identify the nature and dynamics of people's participation as ensured through the efforts of the organisation.
(viii) To attempt an analysis of the nature of leadership evolved in the wake of launching of its programmes.
(ix) To obtain responses of the activists on the functioning of the organisation.
(x) To examine the pattern of its interaction with bureaucracy, development establishments and political parties.
(xi) To elaborate the lessons of its operation in different spheres.
(xii) To isolate variables that account for its achievements and locate factors inhibiting its operation.
(xiii) To elaborate in detail the social consequences of the

implementation of its activities.

(ix) To describe the nature and pattern of network activated for attainment of group goals.

(xv) To explore its strength as an alternative to present model for the amelioration of the condition of the dalits.

(xi) To examine the relevance of such grassroot initiatives for evolving an effective instrument of development and social change.

(xiii) To discuss in detail the spread effect of the conduct of its programme in different settings.

In sum it has been our endeavour to illustrate the characteristic features of the Samiti. We have tried to study the extent to which it has been successful in helping the dalits to graduate from the subject status to the status of citizenship through acquisition of needed social consciousness. The study seeks to elaborate on its strength and weakness at the grassroot level. Through this study we have attempted to find the appropriate fit of goals and strategies that may serve as a model of development.

REFERENCES

1. S.R. Pande, *Community Action for Social Justice*, Sage Publications, New Delhi, 1991, p. 38.
2. D.L. Seth , 'Grassroot Initiatives in India' in *Economic and Political Weekly*, Vol 19, No. 6, 1984, p. 262.
3. Rudolf C. Heredia, *Voluntary Action and Development*, Concept Publishing Company, New Delhi, 1988.
4. Upendra Baxi, 'Activism at Cross roads with Sign Posts, in *Social Action*, Vol 36, 1986, p. 379.
5. Rajni Kothari, "The Non-party Political Process, in *Economic and Political Weekly*, Vol 19, No.5, 1984, p. 220.
6. S.R. Pandey, *op.cit.*, p.205.
7. Rajni Kothari, *op.cit.* p.212.

2

Dalits of Bihar

I

Bihar, the poorest State of India, leads in exploitation of the poor. It is today known more for its failure than for its achievements. It is described as "a stagnant pool in which the scum floats on the top."[1] Semi-feudalism thrives incapacitating the forces of modernity. The gap between accumulation and distribution is the widest in Bihar. Poverty is pervasive and perpetuates with excruciating exploitation of the poor. Caste identities are deeply embedded and influence much of Bihar's 'social-economic and political life'.[2] Bihar tends to be the most unfortunate repository of the brutalities of the caste system. The modifications and differentiation triggered in the wake of interaction between capitalism and semi-feudalism has failed to alter the basic contours of its oppressive social structure. In Bihar caste seems to maintain its presence as "a dead weight holding back not merely the economic and political but also the cultural and moral development of society and even putting its imprint on the new emerging classes".[3] Bihar's affiliation to antiquated norms enshrined in the caste system is firm and ingrained. In 1917, when Gandhiji visited Bihar, adherence to dietary restrictions among upper caste people engaged in secular profession in its capital city is reported to have perturbed him.[4] All his Bihari associates in Champaran, mostly Kayastha lawyers, ran their own kitchen.[5] It was the fear of loosing caste that prevented the Bihari youth from pursuing a medical career.[6] Prior to abolition of *Zamindari*, even the treatment meted out to tenants was affected to a great extent by their location in the ritual hierarchy. The conventional prescription for a Kayastha was to be paid, a Brahmin to be fed, paddy and betal to be watered and lower caste man to be kicked for deriving needed results.[7] The middle range castes were subjected to atrocious treatment for their attempts to 'sanskritize' their life-style. The intermediate castes were not permitted to have the right to wear the sacred thread as it was the prerogative of the twice-born caste.[8]

II

Dalits have been the worst sufferers in the exploitative social order. No sphere of life is such where equality is accorded to them in interaction with superiors in the caste hierarchy. They work on land but cannot claim it, perform services essential to the maintenance of society but are ranked lowest in the traditional hierarchy, produce consumption materials and are rendered untouchables. Segregation and exploitation have been their fate. They have been denied elementary facilities available to members of clean castes and are condemned to live in insularity. They are born in servitude and die in penury. They continue to be peripheral and marginal incapable to claim equality with the privileged. Society remains exploitative, unfair and criminally unjust to them. In rural Bihar, the life of a dalit "is reduced to total dependency on the landlord, since in most places semi-bonded agricultural labour is the only source of livelihood, so also their political life is often reduced to the status of being vote-banks for those who control their lives."[9] The most deprived and down-trodden among the dalits of Bihar are the Musahars who are placed at the margin of subsistence surviving on "rats, snails, snakes or anything else they can find and live in a kind of social thraldom sometime selling themselves and their wives and children to life-long servitude for paltry sums."[10] Dalits are placed unfavourably in the ownership of productive assets as well as the distribution of income. Inequalities tend to be cumulative in their case.

III

One of the institutions for economic exploitation of dalits has been the *Kamia system* reported to be operative in a number of districts in Bihar. "The system seems to have been based on the mechanism of credit and indebtedness. In order to ensure control over labour in time of distress in the post harvest period and in the exceptional times, the rich peasantry would advance small loans to the poor cultivators whereby they secured control over cultivator's labour till repayment of debt was complete."[11] In absence of possession of land, animals and the elementary agricultural inputs, such hapless peasantry could be the most convenient target of the landed castes. Once in debt the poor could not escape from being fleeced by the landlord under the system of bondage. The conditions of debt-repayment were so framed that even the best efforts of the debtor could not ensure his release from the clutches of the landlord. Thus to prevent repayment of debt given to the *Kamia*, the landowners had a condition "that unless it is repaid on a certain day usually sometime in the *Jyeth*, when the funds are low, it is optional for the master to refuse acceptance."[12]

In some of the areas, in addition to 'debt-slavery' a system of bondage nurtured by the caste system has been perpetuated. 'Under this system the landowning upper castes and the labourers belonging to the scheduled caste bind themselves in a life long stable alliance. The bondage is hereditary as it relates to relationship between patrilineal descent groups of masters and servants. As an institution of fairly longstanding it is a "channel to transmit rights and obligations from one generation to another".[13] Under the system the landless labourer turns out to be a transferable commodity sold and mortgaged to settle problem situations.

Landownership is positively related to caste. High status caste possess most of the land while the upper crust among the intermediary castes constitute the middle peasants. Those without land are from lower middle castes and the scheduled castes. Of the four elite castes in Bihar the Rajputs and Bhumihars own the most substantial land and are dominant in the rural areas.[14] Land is unevenly distributed in Bihar. It is more favourably distributed among the small section of the population. Owners of bigger landholdings are small in number. While 73.8 per cent of the population own 21.2 per cent of agricultural land, 26.2 per cent hold 88.8 per cent of land.[15] Tenancy, debt-slavery and usurious exploitation are widespread in Bihar.

Legal provisions for land reforms, in spite of being impressive, has been of little help to dalits on account of tardy implementation. Articulated measures of agrarian reforms have been accorded least priority to ensure their accomplishment in Bihar.[16] The land ceiling acts passed in the sixties and implemented in the seventies have failed to ensure distribution of land identified as surplus. In one of the studies it has been found that only 9.8 per cent of such land could be distributed among the poor on account of large scale evasion in the form of transfer to the 'benamidars.'[17] The law evaders does care a truppence for the administration. Their approach is defiant — their modus operandi ... open and insolent.[18]

Diffusion of new agricultural technology could not benefit dalits in absence of land which is the permissive factor for entitlement to such benefits. Such initiatives failed to elevate them in the economic hierarchy in spite of their contribution in making the programme a success. Output increase failed to benefit the tiller of the soil in the way it added to increase the prosperity of the landowner. The fruits of Green Revolution as achieved under the intensive district agriculture programme failed to trickle downward. In such areas of Bihar where the programme was a success, the prosperous landowners increased their gains "through reneging on or reducing traditional payments to attached labourers in the form of land and grain and through labour displacing tractorisation."[19] The wages in some of the areas remained static. "Increased wages for labour, when reported, generally reflected the prevailing inflated market price for wage in kind and did not increase in rural income for agricultural labourers living at subsistence level."[20] Availability of innovative agricultural inputs has led to large scale displacement of share-croppers by landowners among whom there is a tendency to cultivate land with the help of family members.[21] Commercial agriculture through uneven distribution of benefits has favoured more the landowning caste than those without land.

Specific programmes oriented to poverty alleviation seem to have limited impact in Bihar. Thus the benefits of the scheme launched under the *Antyodaya* programme[22] failed to help the target families in augmenting their income. Integrated rural development could also have limited success in Bihar an account of the failure of the beneficiaries to harness the assets generated for future utilization.[23] The benefits of such schemes is reported to have gone to those who were in a position to manipulate the situation in their own interest. Landless people are reported to be the target of exploitation by the dominant caste groups in milk cooperatives also. The tendency on the part of some to exploit others is strong in Bihar.[24] Dalits are not considered to be credit-worthy. Studies reveal that these people fail to utilize the loans advanced under the special component programme.[25] In Bihar dalits have been benefited least from the development programmes as their share in the development scheme is nominal. In fact programmes aimed at providing relief to poor have "compounded the concentration of powers and patronage and expanded the arena and extent of corruption enhancing the incidence of mis-delivery of the benefits".[26] Poverty alleviation and employment generation tend to be elusive in spite of the operation of programmes wedded to these ends. The relationship between the landowner and the tiller tends to be pre-commercial "having their harshest impact on members of the scheduled castes".[27] The state has failed to ensure payment of minimum wages recommended by it from time to time. The wages have been found to be as low as Rs. 4 a day in many areas of Bihar.[28] This together with the limited days of employment in the village makes it difficult to lift themselves from the condemned life of bondage. Hundreds of landless laboures and poor peasants have been mercilessly killed or have been implicated in false cases to frustrate their claims for the payments due to them. Carnages are perpetrated to scare the labourers asserting for payment of wages at enhanced rate. The poor have little control over productive assets or bargaining power in the labour market. Payment of side payments characteristic of the *Jajmani* system has also been withdrawn. Comprising the deficit sector of economy, dalits remain dependent on loans at exorbitant rate of interest. In the transaction to exploit the poor, the landlords have been reported to be facilitated even by the selfish interests from among the dalits.[29] The replacement of feudal aristocracy by the 'new forward caste', to whom touch of the plough has never been a taboo and who have been directly involved in cultivation, has worsened the situation of dalits. Such landed peasants from the ascendant castes are "more exploitative as they extract more surplus maintaining their exactions by attempting to impose something like a second serfdom infuriating the lower castes".[30] In the semi-feudal agrarian structure, dalits have been forced to live at the margin of subsistence forcing continuance of the "customary need to consume undigested grain picked from the excrement of cattle as they struggle for survival".[31] Aspiring intermediate caste as well as desperate feudal elements tend to be atrociously inclined against dalits.

IV

Caste as a system of hierarchical submission operates as a mechanism of extra-economic coercion of dalits. It contains prescriptions to ensure unrestrained acquiescence of dalits to the caste Hindus by inculcating in them the dominant traits of humbleness. The traditional etiquette had definite political consciousness as it helps in nurturing instincts of submission among the exploited.[32]

> "Qualitative restrictions on consumption and on behaviour have been very much part of caste system. Besides restrictions on consumption the lower castes also faced restrictions like not walking through upper caste *bastis* wearing footwear, or carrying an umbrella. Sitting on a cot in the presence of upper caste persons was also unthinkable. Upper caste names were also taboo for the lower castes or the dalits had perforce to have names like "Dukhi Ram" and so on."[33]

In the prevalent social arrangement dalits were subjected to status disabilities. The values internalised entailed upon dalits the 'solemn duty' to serve the superiors in the caste hierarchy. Such prescriptions could not be challenged. In addition any service received from upper castes was considered sinful and against the arrangement, legitimized in the *Jajmani* system. To quote an instance from Gaya in Bihar:

> "....according to the villagers (the) rule that a low caste should not eat the food of a Brahmin (normally it is the other way about) does not mean retaliation or assertion of equality. It is meant to protect the Brahmin and to enforce due respect for him. Because, if a low caste eats his food, it would not imply contamination, but by cooking for him, the Brahmin's hands might be burnt and cause suffering to him. Within the multicaste village community of Mucharin of today, there is normally no inter-caste dining nor social intercourse even with the upper castes 'unless there is some special occasion when *pukka khana* is served,' this being permitted under the caste rules. But under no circumstances 'would we eat with Harijans'.[34]

Still shameful has been the practices with regard to the sexual exploitation of the women from lower castes. The *dola* system was the name given to the institutionalised sexual exploitation of dalit women. This entitled the landlord to have sex with the newly wed wife of a dalit at his *Kothi*. To quote Indu Bharti:

> "Such was the stranglehold of the feudal order in the village that upper caste landlords were supposed to have an undisputed right over Dalits and Backward caste women. The right had been institutionalised by the landlords through the system of *dola* by which every newly married Dalit woman had to pass her first

night after marriage with the village landlord. Thus those escaped being raped by the landlords had to undergo the trauma after getting married. These were the extra-economic methods devised by the landlords to continuously remind these lower in the caste and class hierarchy of their *aukat*".[35]

The immolation of Mahthin Dai in Behea in whose name there exists a temple represented the culmination of a violent protest movement against sexual exploitation by a King under an institutionalised arrangement. To quote Sinha:

> "Some time ago, there used to be a King by the name Rampal Singh, in Bhojpur whose fiat it was that every newlywed girl be initiated by him. The subjects found this revolting, but did not dare oppose him. One day, Mahthin Dai, a bride refused to go with the King inviting an encounter in which the King was done to death. In the clash also died the husband of Mahthin who then chose to commit *sati*. As a memorial to her bravery, the people built the Mahthin temple at Behea in Central Bhojpur (now Buxar)".[36]

Dalits were not kept in peace during the Hindu festivals. Not only did they lack the means to celebrate, but they were also not entitled to observe them. Festivals meant humiliation to them and their female members. Thus in the celebration to Hindu festival Holi, famous for its vulgarity, it was the dalit women who had the brunt of obscenities hurled at them by upper caste people. The treatment that was meted out to them on such occasions betrayed the helplessness of dalits over the traditionally sanctioned rights available for socially privileged to humiliate their womenfolk. Probably no society in the world accords such latitude to the privileged section. The caste Hindus could arrogate to themselves unlimited latitude to humiliate those having inferior location in the social hierarchy. We cite here a field report from Bihar to illustrate the point made.

> "In the manner in which it used to be observed in Bihar, Holi represented very directly the subjugation of the lower castes, of lower caste women in particular. While the sexually explicit songs would be sung in all *bastis* of the village it was only in the lower caste *bastis* that particular women would be named in the songs.

The lower castes also had their houses splashed with dirt".[37]

The idioms in which the landlords address the untouchable is one of ridicule, abuse and contempt. "Upper castes as well as Yadav and Kurmi landowners persist in treating *Harijans* as inferiors, abusing them in terms such as 'rape-mother' and rape-sister and sexually assaulting Harijan women.[38] The situation was so unfavourable for dalits that in the absence of effective mechanism for redress they found themselves inclined to organise them under leadership of left extremists. The situation that led to the rise of violent uprisings would be evident from the following portrayal of dalits' predicament in Ekwari of Bhojpur. To quote Sinha,

> "Put yourself in the position of a slave in Ekwari and you will understand the urge to reach out for a gun. You are not considered a man at all. Born a slave, your life is strictly tied to spade, sickle and the lord's feet, you produce everything that the lord boasts of. Yet your children are drumming the aluminium plates. Everyday one landlord or other takes away your wife and your daughter. If your working daughter is not spoiled in the fields in the day, the son of the landlord will break into your single room mud hovel in the night, and humiliate her right there. For you the best course is to pretend deep slumber. How long, you will ask yourself, I will take this? Is this my fate".[39]

V

Politically also dalits tend to be of marginal importance. Indifferent to ritual status amongst the colonial rulers failed to prompt them to share power with castes at the bottom of the hierarchy. The Kayasthas, a caste ritually inferior to the three twice born castes enjoyed more influence than other castes. "Bihari Hindus of high social and economic status were somewhat less favoured".[40]

The emergence of the Congress Party led to the emergence of a new elite from the urban educated middle classes.[41] The party, in spite of being "aggregator par excellence", tended to serve the interests of the upper sections of society. Dalits remain by and large neglected. The freedom movement did not "aspire at effective Harijan political mobilisation and politicisation".[42] The leaders exclusively from the ritually superior castes availed unchallenged support of the tertiary sector of the society. The Scheduled Castes on account of lack of education "accepted the Congress leadership and had no desire to form a separate organisation of their own or to have separate leadership ambition of some people."[43] Their plight remained unattended even by the socialist in the Congress who, in spite of being "on the left of the mainstream of the Congress, kept a careful distance from the poor peasants".[44]

During the freedom struggle and thereafter caste has been the most effective force of political mobilisation in Bihar. Primordial instincts and parochial bases constitute the distinguished characteristics in recruitment of support for political ends. Elections to the legislature in the pre-independence phase betrayed the strength of caste to emerge as a base of support-recruitment.[45] Power, however, tended to be confined to the castes at the apex of the caste hierarchy even after attainment of independence and introduction of adult franchise. 'The pattern of recruitment in the Congress (reflected) all basic social divisions in Bihar' ... and a tendency to ensure disproportionate access to power in favour of the upper castes".[46] The one-party dominant system manifested vertical alignment in which middle range castes and untouchables were auxiliaries to the conflicting elites in the upper castes. Ritually superior dominated the numerically strong. In a bid to safeguard its position in the power structure especially from the "upper shudras" the entrenched upper castes "whose leaders although divided by the faction, nevertheless cooperated within the Congress party on the issues affecting the dominance of the upper castes as a whole".[47]

The shifting coalitions among the elite castes tended to perpetuate the Congress monolith.[48] Vertical framework of political organisation in the wake of intensification of political process soon found itself in a situation of opposition from self-assertive intermediate castes indignant against exploitation from the upper castes. The clientist form of politics characterising the initial phase of alignment among the social forces got disturbed. Changes in the eco-structural categories of the elite manifested themselves in the gradual replacement of the entrenched upper castes by the ascendant intermediate castes. However, the shift from upper caste dominated power structure to a situation of ascendancy of middle range castes seem to have failed to ensure a downward percolation of power in favour of dalits. The decline of clientist politics and the change in the elite has failed to bring an end to the context of dependence for dalits leaving them in a situation of inferior existence. In fact "it is only the upper and middle caste groups, with resources of wealth and numbers, that have enjoyed the fruits of caste-oriented democracy while the lower castes have been left for all practical purposes outside the political arena".[49] Castes having peripheral existence are least influential. Politics today in Bihar manifests sharp polarisation between dominant castes and the ascendant castes. Political system, however, tends to be afflicted by inequality of representation as it remains dominated by the upper castes and three intermediate castes.[50] Success in rupture of patron-client network dominated by economically strong and socially superior upper castes has not resulted in acquisition of autonomous political strength among dalits. The shift in locus of power seem to have placed the dalits under the tutelage of the emerging landed castes. The politics of caste pluralism has not favoured dalits to the extent it has helped the numerically strong, economically better and socially privileged intermediate castes. Such plurality in politics remains least significant for caste at the bottom of traditional stratification system.[51] The appropriate status for dalits tend to be follower of the clean castes. Dalits remain adaptive to the social inputs in the political system. In the politics of caste succession leading to the ascendance of the intermediate castes the claim for power tend to be confined in the elite or intermediate castes leaving the untouchables at the periphery.

In spite of the emergence of an elite among dalit castes largely on account of implementation of the policy of protective discrimination the masses among these castes are still "characterised by subject political culture and their participation in the political process is the minimal.[52] Such elite constitute the reference model distinguished from the masses by the modernising impulses and are in a position to guide their unfortunate brethren in embracing the implications of change.[53] In spite of these, the acquisition of modern attributes has not enabled the elite from these castes to claim equality with equally talented but ritually superior caste Hindus. In the context of the larger society Scheduled Caste elites of Bihar represent "privileged untouchables". Then the 'raised up' seem inclined to self-aggrandisement making the collective interest a causality. Such leaders as have the credibility to help interpret and respond to market and state induced inequalities are few and far between. They are reported to be dependent upon more powerful from the upper castes or from the intermediate castes. Leaders from the Scheduled Castes tend to be an appendage of the main contenders in the power structure. The resources acquired by them seem to have enabled them to further their own career interests and material prospects at the cost of their less fortunate dalit brethren. Selfish pragmatism rather than commitment to the cause of dalits, enable the elite to have durable extended elite career.

Peasant mobilisation sponsored by the communists in the organised political sector is reported to have not found much enthusiasm among the dalits as the leaders of such movements are drawn predominantly from the clean castes and "are more empathetic to the cause than to their target of mobilisation".[54] Left orientations in the organised sector of politics in Bihar is reported to have found articulation under the leadership of Bhumihars and such parties are "relatively better organised in areas dominated by this community".[55] Projected ideological orientations acquire less salience in comparison to manifest selfish interest of the leaders. It has been observed that all the party members (of the Communist Party of India) have not joined the party with the view to establish a government of the proletariat rather some of them are taking advantage of the party name to fulfil their own interest.[56]

Failure of the organised sector of politics has spurred the dalits of Bihar to rise in protest against exploitation through spontaneous and sporadic violence. Such assertions comprising striving in the unorganised sector of politics have in course of time and in spite of retaliations have acquired institutionalisation with explicit strategies under effective leadership. These uprisings 'representing the limelight zone between organised and unorganised political sector are now widespread in Bihar. The left outfits find support among dalits in distress and have acquired organisational cohesion and strategic direction from distinct urban middle class radical leadership.[57] Ideologically wedded support pattern that seems to replace the patron-client alignment has rendered cohesion and independence to dalits as a political force. The leadership even in such organisations however tends to be elusive as far as Scheduled Castes are concerned. Since the cost involved in failure of the violent protest is high and the likely benefits minimal there are occasions when dalits tend to be apathetic, inert and passive to such initiatives. Socio-economic configuration of poverty inhibits mobilisation of the rural poor. In extreme cases dalits tend to remain 'a conquered population split up and dispersed by individual attachment among the conquerors.'[58] Apathy or anomie among these poor are what Rudolph[59] calls 'rational adaptations' in a culture characterised by destitution and discrimination.

REFERENCES

1. Arvind N. Das 'A Lost Cause' in *Economic and Political Weekly*, Vol 12, No. 17, 1987, p. 737
2. Atul Kohli, *Democracy and Discontent*, Cambridge University Press, New York, 1991
3. DN 'Problems of Unity in the Agrarian Struggle' in *Economic and Political Weekly*, Vol 23, No 19, 1988, p. 194
4. G.D. Tendulker, *Gandhi in Champaran*.
5. V.C.P. Chaudhury, *The Creation of Modern Bihar*.
6. V.C.P. Chaudhury, *op.cit.*
7. George Grierson, *Bihar Peasant Life*, Cosmo Publications, Delhi 1975
8. Marcus Franda , *Small is Politics*, Wiley - Eastern Limited, New Delhi, 1979
9. Jose Kananaikil, 'Marginalisation of the Scheduled Castes' in *Scheduled Castes and the Struggle Against Inequality* edited by Jose Kananaikil, Indian Social Institute, New Delhi, 1983 p.62.
10. J. Byrne, *Bengal District Gazetters : Bhagalpur*, Government of Bengal, Calcutta, 1911, p. 52
11. Manoshi Mitra, *Agrarian Social Structure*, Manohar, New Delhi.
12. Radhakamal Mukerjee, *Land Problems of India*, London, 1961
13. A.K. Lal, *Politics of Poverty*, Chetana Publications, New Delhi, 1977.
14. Marcus Frands, *op.cit* p. 249
15. Pradhan H. Prasad, Agrarian Violence in Bihar in *Economic and Political Weekly*, Vol 12, No. 32, 1987
16. Pradip K. Bose, "Mobility and Conflict: Social Roots of Caste Violence in Bihar," in *Social Stratification* edited by Dipankar Gupta, Oxford India, Paperback, New Delhi, 1993.
17. Sachchidananda, *The Harijans in Bihar*, Paper Presented at Seminar on "Social Realities in Bihar, February 26-28, 1986 A.N. Sinha Institute of Social Studies, Patna.
18. Mohan Ram, 'The Sarvodhya Force' in *Economic and Political Weekly*, May 1975.
19. Paul Brass, *The Politics of India Since Independence*, Cambridge University Press, Orient Longman, Hyderabad, 1990, p. 302.
20. F. Tomassan Januzi, *Agrarian Crisis in India*, Sangam Books, New Delhi, 1974
21. M.N. Karna "Agrarian Tension and Violence" in *Journal of Social and Economic Studies*, Vol 13, No 1, March, 1975.
22. K.K. Sinha, *Antyodaya and Development*, A.N. Sinha Institute of Social Studies, Patna, 1987 (mimeo).
23. Rajan Verma, *I.R.D.P. Among the Harijans and Adivasis in Bihar*, A.N. Sinha Institute of Social Studies, Patna, 1987 (mimeo).
24. M. Mitra 'Anand in Bihar: Replication of Caste and Class Patterns' in *Resources Institutions and Strategies* edited by Martin Dornbos and K.N. Nair, Sage Publications, New Delhi, 1990.
25. Anirudh Prasad, *Impact of the Special Component Plan among the Harijans in Bihar*, 1986 (mimeo).
26. L.C. Jain, *Grass without Roots*, Sage Publications, New Delhi, 1981.
27. Atul Kohli, *op.cit* p. 203.
28. Indu Bharati, 'Force of Farm Wage Hike' in *Economic and Political Weekly*, Vol 15, No. 8, 1990, p. 1512

29. A.K. Daftuar, *Indebtedness among Harijans in Bihar*, A.N. Sinha Institute of Social Studies, Patna, 1983 (mimeo).
30. Atul Kohil, *op.cit.*
31. F. T. Januzi, *op.cit.*
32. Barrington Moore, *Social Origins of Dictatorship and Democracy*, Hermandsworth, 1984
33. DN 'Changes in Holi in Bihar' in *Economic and Political Weekly*, Vol 14, No. 5, 1989 p. 231
34. Kusum Nair, *Blossoms in the Dust*, Gerald Duckworth and Co. Ltd, London, 1964.
35. Indu Bharti 'Dalits Gain New Izzat' in *Economic and Political Weekly*, Vol 15, 18-19, 1990, p. 980
36. Arun Sinha, 'The Awakening in Bhojpur' in *Naxalbari and After*, edited by Samir Sen *et al*, Kathashilpa, Calcutta, 1978 p. 73.
37. DN, 'Changes in Holi in Bihar, in *Economic and Political Weekly*, Vol 14, No. 5, 1989, p. 231.
38. Francine R. Frankel, 'Caste, Land and Domination in Bihar' in *Dominance and State Power in Modern India*, edited by Francine R. Frankel and M.S.A. Rao, Oxford India, Paperback, New Delhi, 1993.
39. Arun Sinha, *op cit*, p. 296
40. F. T. Januzi, *op cit.*
41. B.B. Mishra, *The Indian Middle Classes*, Oxford University Press, 1960.
42. M.P. Singh, *Cohesion in a Predominant Party*, S. Chand, New Delhi, 1978.
43. Rajendra Prasad, *Autobiography*, Asia Publishing House, New Delhi, 1952
44. Stephen Hennigham, Autonomy and Organisation, in *Economic and Political Weekly* Vol. 16, No 27, 1981, p. 1153.
45. O'Mallay L.S.S. *Indian Caste Customs*, Cambridge University Press, Cambridge, 1932
46. Ramashray Roy, Caste and Political Recruitment in Bihar' in *Caste in Indian Politics*, edited by Rajni Kothari, Orient Longman, New Delhi, 1970.
47. Francine, Frankel, *op cit*, p. 47
    Paul Brass, *op cit*, p.67
48. F.T. Januzi, *op cit*, p. 159
49. Harry W. Blair, *Voting Caste Community and Society*, Young Asia Publishers, New Delhi, 1979
50. Paul Brass, *op. cit*, p.18
51. Harry W. Blair, *op cit*, p.177
52. Marcus Franda, *op cit.*
53. A.K. Lal, 'The Educated Harijans as Elite' in *Elite and Development* edited by Sachchidananda and A.K. Lal, Concept Publishing Company, New Delhi, 1980.
54. T.K. Oommen, *Protest and Change*, Sage Publications, New Delhi, 1990 p. 269
55. Paul Brass, *op cit*, p. 67.
56. Gulab Jha, *Caste and the Communist Movement*, Commonwealth Publishers, New Delhi, 1990.
57. Stephen Hennigham, *op cit*, p. 1152
58. A.K. Lal, *Politics of Poverty*, Chetana Publications, New Delhi, 1977
59. L.L. Rudolph and S.H. Rudolph , *In Pursuit of Lakshmi*, Orient Longman, New Delhi, 1987, p. 387.

3

The Samiti and its Activists

I

The Samiti represents the formalisation of an action research programme originally initiated by the Indian Social Institute in the early eighties. Its creation marks the inauguration of a new initiative for emancipation of dalits in Bihar. The institute launched a programme for integrated growth of the Barh and Pandarak blocks in the district of Patna. The selection of the area was purposive as it had heavy concentration of the scheduled castes living uncared under a situation of exploitation. The approachability of the area from Patna was the other consideration for its selection.

The founder leader of organisation is Dr. Jose Kananaikil, a Jesuit scholar from Kerala, who had made Bihar his *Karmabhumi*. Dr. Kananaikil is a sociologist of repute who obtained a Ph.D. degree in Sociology from Chicago for his thesis on the problems of the Scheduled Castes. He was not only familiar to the place but also had deep rapport with dalits of the area whom he first knew while conducting his field work. In addition to being an excellent piece of dalit sociology, the study itself turned out to be 'a reflection of leadership building process for dalits' involving in its wake Dr. Kananaikil as a leader totally dedicated to the task. The action Sociologist in him first received nationwide attention on September 20, 1983 when he filed a writ petition in the Supreme Court against the Government of Bihar for its refusal to register a case of mass rape and assault. Earlier he had organised dalits to get them federated to share their pains and pleasure together. The inspiring words of this man led a few among the dalits to get themselves organised under his leadership. This informal federation of people operated as initiator of mass awakening programme among the dalits of the area. This was the time when Dr. Kananaikil had to get himself involved rather deeply to secure justice for the unfortunate victims of mass rape in Babubigha. This initiative on his part found sustenance in the diverse activities for the dalits to help them come out of the morass of degradation. Originally it was known as 'Harijan Uthan Samiti' but subsequently in order to incorporate poor people especially from among the *Upper Shudras* it acquired the name of "Bihar Dalit Vikas Samiti". The founder leader helped the Samiti to acquire a formalised and stable structure to conduct its programmes. The alignment among the activists is professional rather than personal. The leader is to the activists and the masses a great soul and is held in reverence and with gratitude. To the dalits of the area he is a saint respectfully called as *baba*. His messages are to be found on the walls in the villages. He is recipient of many awards including the national award of Bhartiya Dalit Sahitya Academy.

II

As on December 1992, there were more than one hundred volunteers attached to the organisation. They are placed at 14 centres. There were 588 registered village units catering to the needs of 27508 individuals.

Conscientised adults from the lower castes and their affiliates from other places constitute the support structure of the organisation. It is a sociologist-initiated formal structural organisation having a support structure evolved through nurturing of the pre-existing linkages among the people. It has a decentralised structure guaranteeing autonomy to spatially differentiated without loosing the inter-sectoral choesion. Distance between leaders and members is minimal. It has led to emergence of leaders from its ranks. The activists work as catalysts or animators. The units do not operate in insularity. Their endeavours are coordinated and strengthened to help emergence of a viable social movement.

Each centre seems to have been started with the help of a small number of social workers. The strength of volunteers has been raised with the passage of time and expansion of activities. The number of volunteers placed at different centres seem to be by and large constant once the centre is supposed to have reached the take-off stage. Taking up of new time-bound and target-specific programmes seem to have led to temporary addition to the strength of volunteers. However, such additional hands are withdrawn as soon as the task is accomplished.

Barh, the headquarters of the Samiti has the largest number of volunteers. Its performance has also been impressive interms of programmes and their coverage. There is, however, no positive relationship between the strength of the volunteers and number of village units affiliated. This is probably on account of the fact that the volunteers placed at centres with only a few village units have to shoulder other important functions putting a gloss to task of unit formation.

III

The Samiti has both male as well as female workers. The male workers are more numerous than the female workers. 83.2 per cent of the workers are male while the females have representation to the tune of 16.8 per cent. For the section characterised by ignorance, poverty and illiteracy this is not a mean achievement. It goes to the credit of the Samiti that it has found at least a few female workers without whose involvement in the programme its concern for uplift of dalit including its women would have remained unattended. Female workers have better chance of acceptance among the women than their male counterparts. Structuring them into the role of social works represents important contribution for which the Samiti deserves credit.

Social workers requires the active involvement of youths. While old and experienced are important as source of inspiration and guidance, it is the youth who are more suitable to take pains and encounter hostilities. Old people are less prone to take risks. They are also likely to be more in tune with the traditionally established behavioural patterns. Such orientations cannot facilitate efforts to question the *status quo*. The Samiti seems to be alive to this fact. Among its activists, there is the dominance of persons in the working age group. The largest section is constituted of those who are in the age category 21 to 30 years. They account for 48.5 per cent of the activists in the Samiti. They are followed by persons in the age category 31 to 40 years who account for 35.5 per cent of the strength of social workers in the Samiti. Those who are past forty are few and far between. All the heads of the centre are young people.

Education is sparse among the Scheduled Caste. This is because of their traditional occupations which require little education. Encouragement to education was minimum in absence of resources. Then educated among such people are inclined to have the settled life of an employed man than to be in social work. The same is true of people having proximate social status with the Scheduled Castes. This being the case the chances of having educated persons as social workers are negligible among the dalits. This is corroborated from the analysis of the educational profile of the dalits entrusted with the task of social work in the Samiti. Thus the majority of the social workers i.e. 51.3 per cent are such who have read up to matriculation. This is, however, not to construe that highly educated people among the dalits do not appear fascinated to social work. Thus as many as 25.2 per cent of the social workers are such who are graduates. Similarly 18.6 per cent of the social workers have obtained intermediate degrees. Highly educated and illiterate persons constitute negligible representation among the workers.

The membership to the Samiti is not confined to any particular religion. Poor people from different religious groups have found representation among the social workers. As many as 64.5 per cent of the social workers are Hindus. The next in strength are those who are Christians. They account for 33.6 per cent of the total social workers. There is negligible representation of the Muslims as they account for 1.9 per cent of the total social workers.

We have also attempted to clássify the social workers on the basis of the caste to which they belong. It is evident that the overwhelming majority of the social workers are from the Scheduled Castes. Such workers account for nearly 87.3 per cent of the social workers. Among the Scheduled Castes the Chamars have the largest number of social workers in the Samiti. They account for 55.4 per cent of the total social workers. The next in strength happen to be Dusadhs who comprise 20.5 per cent of the social workers. The Pasis have negligible representation like the Musahars. The sparse representation of the Musahars is natural as they are still steeped in inertia. Intermediate castes have also found representation among the social workers however their strength is poor.

The association with this organisation has been recent in the cases of a few castes. Thus while the Chamars, Dusadhs and Pasis have been inducted from the very inception other castes' interest in the organisation is not that old. Among the different Scheduled Castes Mushars and Dhobis have been involved after the Samiti could work for some time. Other castes having sparse representation among the social workers have not been inducted at all the different phases of the expansion of the organisation. Their recruitment to the Samiti does not manifest the regularity that is evident in the cases of Chamar, Dusadh and Pasi who together comprise the bulk of the social workers of the Samiti.

We have also tried to analyse the compositional types of families to which the social workers belong. We have obtained their responses to classify them into different categories. As many as 52.3 per cent of the respondents are members of the joint families. Among these the largest number (24.3%) is constituted of those who are members of lineal-collateral joint families. Next is the strength of such joint families as are only lineal in character. They account for 21.5 per cent of the families. Such joint families as have members other than linear-collateral families have 6.5 per cent representation in the sample. The tendency for living jointly with the families of the same generation is not prominent. Only 2.8 per cent of the social workers are members of collateral joint families. Among the different categories of the families for which the responses have been collected, the nuclear families appears to be the most numerous. Thus as many as 26.1 per cent of the social workers are members of the nuclear families. In spite of considerable nuclearisation in the family there is an inclination for having additional members to supplement such nuclear families. We have social workers from sub-nuclear families also and such social workers have 6.5 per cent representation in the sample. While summing up the discussion it may be maintained that complete nuclearisation of the family is not the dominant characteristics among the dalits. They have a tendency to live with members other than those comprising their own nuclear families.

We have obtained figures on the occupational status of the different male members of families of the social workers associated with the Samiti. The figures in this regard indicate that 93.5 per cent of the social workers are members of such families which have other earning male members. This in other words means that stipend made available from the Samiti is not the only source of income for their families. The figures indicate that as many as 49.5 per cent of the social workers are in receipt of monetary support from at least one male member of the family. Such social workers who have two earning male members in their family account for 31.7 per cent of the social workers. This is also clear that families having more than three earning male members (including the respondents) are few and far between. Such social workers as have 3 additional earning male members have the strength of 9.3 per cent while those who have 4 additional earning male members constitute 2.8 per cent of the social workers. We have also obtained figures on the employment status of the females belonging to the families of the social workers. The figures in this regard suggests that the majority is constituted of such families where females do not work for wages. Such families have 68.2 per cent representation in the sample. In contrast to these 31.7 per cent of the respondents are members of such families where females also earn.

In most of the cases only one female has been reported to be earning to support the family. There is only one family where 2 females have been reported to be earning. This indicates that there is a withdrawal of the womenfolks from the manual work of agriculture. So far as social workers families are concerned, they constitute the privileged section among the stratum that occupies the base of the caste hierarchy. Education and elevation of their occupational status as social workers of the Samiti tends to be inimical to the practice of allowing women in agricultural operations. Such being the case there seems to be an immediate need to equip the females of such families in modern skills for earning income.

IV

The Samiti is engaged in a number of tasks. In order to accomplish the tasks it has organised its workers into different departments. There is however a frequent change in the assignments of the social workers. This is done to accord them familiarity with requirements of different tasks to which the Samiti is wedded. Thus 54.3 per cent of the social workers are such who have experiences of work in more than one department. As many as 23.3 per cent of the social workers are such who have reported to have worked in two departments. Similarly 14.0 per cent have worked in three departments. This is followed by those who have worked in four departments. They account for 12.1 per cent of the social workers. A small number of social workers have experience of handling five different activities of the organisation. It is also to be noted that in the case of 45.7 per cent of the social workers there has been no change in the assignments. Thus it can be said that there is a tendency in the organisation to provide opportunities to the social workers to have expertise in different activities of the Samiti.

An attempt was made to study the pattern of recruitment of the social workers to the Samiti. It seems that many of the social workers have been inducted to organisation with the help of the resource network available to them. 61.6 per cent of the social workers got inducted to the organisation through the action set in which workers already attached to the Samiti constituted the primary star zone. Thus, in the bulk of the cases, the recruitment seem to have been made through the connections existing in the Samiti. There are instances where persons have through their own initiatives approached the office bearers of the Samiti to get them recruited as social workers. Such social workers have the strength of 26.1 per cent. There are a few social workers whose relatives helped them in their induction to the Samiti. Such social workers have the strength of 9.3 per cent. In their case the primary position in the action set for induction in the Samiti happened to be pre-existing ties to kinship. It would be also interesting to note that such social workers as have relatives in the organisation are confined to only five places while workers that have found entry through their own initiatives or through their linkages with other workers in the organisation have dispersed existence in the Samiti.

It would be interesting to note that a number of social workers are such whose relatives are also working in the organisation. Such social workers account for 33.4 per cent of the social workers. Thus as many as 6.5 per cent of the social workers have their sibling in the Samiti. At least 2 (1.8%) are such who are having their parents in the Samiti. Secondary relatives are more in strength than the primary relatives. Tertiary relatives however constitute the largest category of relative reported to be working in the organisation. They have the strength of 15.8 per cent.

We have studied affiliation of the social workers with other organisations. It is evident that as many as 90.6 per cent of the social workers are exclusively affiliated to the Samiti. Among such respondents as have association with other organisations 3 social workers (2.8%) are members of statutory village council (village Panchayat). The remaining 7 are affiliated to different organisations. Thus it is clear that the social workers seem to be totally dedicated to the tasks of the Samiti.

The association of the social workers with the activities of the Samiti has also helped them in development of their own personality. This is corroborated from the fact that 69.1 per cent of the social workers have indicated that the organisation has accorded individual benefits to the social workers. As many as 24.3 per cent of the social workers indicate that their stay in the organisation has helped them in acquiring higher education. 53.2 per cent are of the opinion that association with the Samiti has helped them in elevation of their social status. 5.6 per cent of the social workers have found the Samiti conducive to increase in their political consciousness. Two of the social workers have indicated that the Samiti made them conscious to the need of having a smaller family. They in fact went for adoption of family planning measures. The Samiti has been reported to have helped 2 social workers in augmenting their income through expansion of their personal business.

An analysis of the period of association of the social workers with the Samiti indicates that they have been inducted at different periods of time. It seems that recruitment for the social work in the Samiti is a continuous process. In every year there seems to be addition to the existing strength. Among the workers are included persons having different length of experience. Thus the majority of the social workers are such who have spent more than 4 years in the organisation. Such workers as have very long stay in the organisation are few and far between. The largest category is constituted of those who have completed 5 years of social work in the Samiti. Their strength is followed by those who have completed 4 years of stay in the organisation while the former account for 16.8 per cent of the respondents, the latter has the strength of 14.9 per cent. Such social workers as have been inducted during the last 3 years have also significant representation in the Samiti. Thus those who have completed 2 years of association with the organisation account for 11.2 per cent of total workers. Similarly, those who have completed their first year of social work in the Samiti account for 10.2 per cent of the social workers. Such social workers as are in the initial phase account for 10.2 per cent of the social workers. It is also evident that social workers with more than 7 years of experience are in minority.

If we correlate the length of association of the social workers with the place where they are operative we find that experienced workers are in a highly dominant strength in Barh. Other places do not have social workers with that length of experience in such number. However, experienced social workers are to be found in many of the centres including Saharsa, Samastipur, Khagaria and Fatuha. Other places have social workers that seem to be recently inducted to conduct the programmes of the Samiti.

We have tried to find out a correlation between the age of social workers with their duration of association in the organisation. The figures in this regard indicate that such social workers as are below 20 years of age have the maximum duration of stay of 3 years. Social workers in the age category of 21 to 30 years have been working for longer period. Thus 19.3 per cent of such workers have worked for 6 years. The next is the strength of such social workers in this age category as have worked for 2 years. They account for 17.3 per cent of the social workers in this age category. Those from this age category as have reported to have worked for 3 years have the strength of 15.3 per cent. 9.6 per cent of social workers from this age category have been reported to be associated with the organisation for 5 years. Those who have worked for four years constitute 7.6 per cent of the social workers in this age category. Identical is the case of those from this age category which have reported to have worked for 7 years. While 3.8 per cent of such social workers have worked for 8 years, those who have worked for 10 years constitute 5.7 per cent of the social workers in this age category. There is one person in this age category that has worked for more than 10 years.

Such social workers as have been recently inducted in the organisation are young in most of the cases. Thus 54.5 per cent of the social workers associated only for one year in the organisation come from the age category of 21 to 30 years. This is followed by those who are above 30 years but have not crossed 40 years of age. These persons have 33.3 per cent representation among those who have been recently inducted. Only one social worker comprising 9 per cent of the respondents in this age group is such as has not attained the age of 20 years. It is further evident that 81.8 per cent of respondents who have completed 2 years of their association in the organisation belong to the age category 21 to 30 years. Other age groups find negligible representation in the category of social workers. It is evident that age is positively correlated with period of association. This does not mean that all the social workers having long experience of association in the Samiti are old people. However, older people are more to be found among such social workers as have work experience of more than 4 years.

We tried to obtain a classification of the social workers according to the stipend paid to them by the Samiti. Eighty per cent of the social workers are the recipient of high stipends. Thus 35.5 per cent get monthly stipend between Rs. 801-1000. Their position is followed by those who get more than Rs. 1100 as their monthly stipend. Such social workers have 26.1 per cent representation. Among the social workers those who have monthly stipend between Rs. 1001-1200 have not insignificant representation in the sample. They have the strength of 18.6 per cent. Such social workers as have Rs.600 or less as their monthly stipend have 8.4 per cent representation in the sample and those whose monthly stipend is between Rs. 601-800 have 11.2 per cent of strength.

It would be interesting to note here that there is great dissatisfaction amongst social workers over the amount paid to them as their monthly stipend. This is but natural as the payment rceeived from the Samiti constitute the main income for their livelihood. With this slender income they seem to find it difficult to maintain their family. Many educated persons do not in all the cases happen to be the recipients of high stipend. Amount of stipend seems to be more a function of other factors particularly the length of association. However, educated persons are in majority of the cases better placed than those having little education. Those who have done their graduation are recipients of high stipend in majority of the cases. But among these a number of social workers are such who receive a stipend available to a simple literate or sparsely educated social worker.

97.2 per cent of the social workers have expressed that the stipend provided is not to their satisfaction. The remaining 3 social workers who account for 2.8 per cent of the total strength feel satisfied.

It is further interesting to note that in spite of their dissatisfaction as many as 39.0 per cent of the workers are willing to work on the prevalent rate of stipend while 58.8 per cent of the workers have expressed their unwillingness to continue with the Samiti at the prevalent rate of stipend.

In the course of their interview a number of social workers complained about the problem of their frequent shifting. They maintained that on account of this at times it becomes difficult to have adequate familiarity of the situation. Such frequent transfers they maintain, also leave many of the programmes incomplete in the manner conceived by the social workers. This however, does not find corroboration from the figures on shifting of social workers. Such social workers as have been shifted to more than three places are in minority as they account for 15.8 per cent of the total workers. The largest number of respondents have been shifted only once. They account for 33.6 per cent of the social workers. Such social workers as have work experience at three places have the strength of 25.2 per cent. Identical is the strength of such social workers as have work experience of only one place. Transfers of social workers to different places seem inevitable as new place have to be covered. This is also necessary to meet special requirements.

It is also evident that there is positive correlation between length of association and frequency of transfers. Such persons as have less than 5 years of experience have been shifted not more than twice. Similarly among those who have experience of work at more than 3 places bulk comprise such social workers as are in the Samiti for more than 7 years. It is also interesting to note that there are social workers who in spite of being associated with the Samiti for more than 7 years have not been shifted even once. But they are in negligible numbers.

4

Legal Aid for Dalits

I

Provision of legal aid happened to be the primary strategy of the Samiti for the upliftment of dalits in the initial phase. This tends to be the most effective strategy employed by the Samiti to equip the dalits in their struggle for the due guaranteed to them under the constitution.

Dalits are unfavourably placed in the matter of seeking justice available to them under the provisions of the Constitution. Access to law is difficult for them. The provisions to safeguard them against exploitation tend to be elusive in their case. The gap between the poor and the legal institution is wide. Ignorance of legal provisions incapacitates them. They are unable to use law not only their perpetual exploitation. Ignorance tends to "narrow people's perception about their inequitable past but also act as a damper preventing the emergence of needs and expectations".[1] They also seem unable to provide any systematic input of their problems in the court system in a proactive manner. The judiciary on account of its self-imposed insularity tends to be cloistered. The 'interpretation and manipulation of interpretation' are not easily accessible to the poor.[2] The laws are so complex that they are subjected to manipulation in the process of interpretation. These remain strange to a common villager in the face of the bureaucratic complexities.[3] Lower castes even though they are aware of the provisions and are conscious could hardly be a match to the manipulation of legal system by the privileged section of the society. The latter with their better status intimate familiarity with the culture of litigation and intricacies of law and deep rapport with officials are well placed, strategically as well as resourcefully. Poverty is the greatest bottleneck to seek redress under an expensive system of adjudication. The poor cannot afford repeated court appearances. Once activated, law should have sustained involvement of the complainant for its ultimate culmination. To hold it out longer one has to be financially sound. Dalits are also constrained due to lack of willing support of witnesses. Such witnesses from their own community are often vulnerable to intimidation and reprisal. "Very often they are economically dependant upon the higher castes. They may face social boycott or reprisal in the form of eviction or denial of grazing rights where they not meet with physical coercion in the form of beatings".[4] In many cases it is considered culturally unnatural "to turn at once to lawyer's law for redress of grievances. It is either the last or an inescapable resort".[5] Then there are issues that are considered insulated areas for litigation. Thus law and the legal personnel are considered to be oppressive to dalits. In fact the legal system, by and large, remains an effective mechanism of socio-economic control. Informal micro level organisation have emerged to make law inaccessible to dalits.

Such dalits, therefore, are in need of legal aid. The availability of "equal legal service as much to the weak and in want as to the strong and affluent and dispensation of social justice through the legal order constitutes the objective of legal aid".[6] It is needed to ensure justice to the deprived section of the community. The Samiti has been an effective mechanism to extend legal facilities to the poor and their unrepresented interests. Its steps to initiate a system of delivery of legal service is aimed at helping the process of social transformation.

II

One of the most important achievements of the legal aid cell of the Samiti was its success in a public interest litigation which sought punishment for the culprits of rape and dacoity committed against the Scheduled Castes of Babubigha in June 1983. The atrocities were shameful. The initial quest for justice was repeatedly frustrated on account of the efforts of manipulative culprits and insensitive administration adding insult to injury. The guilty of Babubigha could be punished only because of the intervention of Dr. Kananaikil, the founder of the Samiti. The details in this connection are given below.

"What took place on June 10, 1983 was a horrible tale of human cruelty. The 15-odd Harijan families still shudder to think of that darkest night in their lives. Some 40 to 50 fire spitting, marauding *goondas* descended upon their village in the dead of the night, to let loose a region of terror. When they left, Babubigha looked like a deserted ancient Indian village pillaged by some ruthless invaders: old men with broken limbs, able-bodied gagged and strapped to their own *charpais* (cots); children too numb with fright even to cry, and women both young and old, the worst sufferers, bleeding and in agony, some unconscious and others trying desperately to hide their shame. It was as if a devil of destruction had passed over the village.

Parvati Kumar (14) unmarried, was sleeping at the door of her hut with her grand-mother when she was rudely awakened by some strange men and was dragged inside. Her father who came to her rescue was dealt with severe blows with iron rods. He fell unconscious and was left for dead. What followed then was a scene straight out from Indian cinema. Recounting her harrowing experience later to a group of college girls from Patna, Parvati said "Some caught my hands another my feet and they gagged me. The, three of them raped me"

Another victim, Lalti Devi, married for five years and three months pregnant was aborted due to the insane acts of the men. "They also took away everything," she wept before the sympathising girls, "clothes, utensils, fowls, goats and money". What they were left with were the clothes on their backs—that too torn and smeared with blood.

The attackers went on with a definite plan. They tried to inflict maximum damage to the people's psyche. In their mad frenzy they did not even spare women with little kids. Kerva, mother of three, was fast asleep in her hut with her children cuddled around her, when the men broke in, and she had no defence against them. Throwing her children out, they gangraped her, while one of them stood on guard outside the house.

Similar, was the fate of Sudamia, wife of Ram Preet Das, Her pleas to leave her alone fell on deaf ears as she fell victim to the men's lust. "I begged them to take away everything and leave me alone, but they said they had come especially to rape me". Even the old women could not escape. Fifty year old Janki Devi said she was raped once and allowed to go when one of the dacoits flashed his torch on her face and exclaimed loudly that she was an old woman and why his friends should waste their time on her. Some seven women were raped each one by four or five men. Three of them were unmarried and in their teens. Out of the four married women, two had been pregnant and lost their babies as a result of the rape.

In the first letter written to Dr. Jose Kananaikil at the Indian Social Institute, New Delhi, some mentions had been made about the landlords behind this crime. However, later investigations revealed that the attackers came mainly from the village, the Beldar community. The Beldars constituted a large community of more than 200 families. Although they are a backward community and not very rich, they are accustomed to receiving services from the Harijan community, free of charge. The study conducted by Dr. Jose Kananaikil revealed that the only reason behind the ghastly crime of June 10, 1983, was the fact that the Harijans had begun to act more and more independently and were refusing to serve the Beldars freely and to be at their beck and call. They wanted to teach the Harijans "a lesson". The criminals who were involved in the crime of June 10, 1983 were found roaming around the village, commenting in Hindi "Now that you have learnt a lesson, you will know how to behave".

Meanwhile, they had heard of Dr. Jose Kananaikil of the Indian Social Institute, New Delhi, working in the Barh area. The people also wrote to him. In the letter they had narrated the incident and explained how inhumanly they were treated at the local level. On getting the letter, Dr. Jose Kananaikil consulted his colleague P.D. Mathew and together they contacted Justice P.N. Bhagwati, Chairman of the Committee for Implementing Legal Aid Schemes (CILAS), New Delhi. They narrated the gross harassment and atrocities committed upon the Harijans of Babubigha. The letter was treated as a writ petition on July 26, 1983. Notices were issued. Dr. Jose Kananaikil rushed to Bihar to visit the village and to inform the people.

All the efforts of the local authorities to colour the case and give it a new twist failed miserably before a sympathetic judiciary which did not entertain any excuses and the determined people who were encouraged by the new turn of events pursued the matter rigorously and intelligently. The State Government had to bend before the new awakening among the people. It did not dilly-dally with the arrest of the accused. All the eleven were soon brought behind the bars. It then informed the court that it has filed criminal cases against all those alleged to have committed dacoity and raped the women.[7]

The Samiti also took up the case of a dalit whose eyes were damaged on account of his opposition to the exploitation of the landlords, one of whom had kept his cousin in bondage. The incident was narrated in a news magazine as below:-

> "When police poured acid into the eyes of a few in Bhagalpur a couple of years back, the world gasped. Things have not changed much since then. If it has not been the police either the quacks or the goons, who abound in Bihar, are blinding people every year. Take the case of Ram Swaroop Das. He is young, 25, plays an instrument in a village band and is bold. On February 11, at about 3 p.m. he along with his friend Lakhan Das stopped outside a toddy shop. Lakhan Das asked for toddy. But a shopkeeper from the neighbouring shop appeared and asked them why they were making noise. He then produced a pistol. Seeing this both Ram Swaroop and Lakhan Dan ran and hid in a nearby house.
>
> They were soon traced. Ram Swaroop was taken to the house of a strongman, of the village. Here they tied him to a *charpai* and beat him ruthlessly. After this four or five men held a meeting and it was decided to gorge out Swaroop's eyes. "They untied me and pierced my eyes several times", Ram Swaroop told *The Week*.
>
> He was then taken to the thana and a false case of dacoity and theft was lodged against him. Brijnandan's men told the police that Ram Swaroop had a pistol. Mr. Swaroop is a Chamar (shoemaker) by caste and hails from Manjhala Bigha, Block Pandarak, Patna district, 45 miles away from Patna where the incident took place. The village is dominated by Yadavas.
>
> Why was Swaroop blinded? Brijnandan Yadav has two bonded labourers working for him, one of whom happened to be Ram Swaroop's cousin. Ram Swaroop used to demand that his cousin be freed from bondage. He always spoke out boldly and had shown signs of leadership in the village.
>
> Thus, the Yadavas were determined to silence him. The two bonded labourers had been working for Brijnandan for years and had already paid back Rs. 600 which their forefathers had borrowed

from Brijnandan's family. But the latter still accused the two labourers of owing him Rs. 7,500 and was not prepared to release them.

There are a few police cases pending against Ram Swaroop but to what extent these cases are genuine, is still to be proved. The fact remains that even in police custody, he was beaten. He received two injections and was bandaged in a dental clinic in the village while his eyes got worse. He remained in lock-up for four days. On February 16, he was brought to the Kurji Holy Family Hospital, Patna where doctors tried their best to restore his eyesight".[8]

Among dalits there often have been persons to whom exploitation by the landlords was unacceptable. Such persons helped other dalits in seeking redemption from the fetters of exploitation. Landowners, on the other hand have always resisted such attempts. There have been occasions when the rising voice of discontent has been silenced for ever by elimination of leadership in pursuit of such ends. We cite an incident that led the Smiti to get itself associated in helping dalits in their fight against exploitation :

"In Chak Jalalpur village which is under the Pandarak development block a dalit named Shankar Paswan was emerging as a powerful leader of dalits. He led dalits in their revolts against the landlords. He helped them to struggle for minimum wages and stirred them to seek an end to their exploitation. In the month of January 1980, while returning from the local court he was brutally killed by the landlords. This incident was in a process of being hushed up. The Samiti at that time operative from Delhi took up the case. The killers of Shanker Paswan were sentenced to life imprisonment."

III

The poor and innocent people are often subjected to harassment by the police. This is because of the fact that they are ignorant and lack the resource to save themselves from the implicating clutches of the police. The Samiti has been quite helpful to such innocent people. We cite here an instance:

"In one of the villages in *Daniwan* the Manjhis are involved in illicit preparation of liquor. A few among the Manjhis are involved in crimes also. In the year 1993 a man belonging to Chamar caste was killed. In the course of investigation it was found that the son of one of the Manjhis is responsible for the murder. Instead of arresting the culprit the police implicated a minor boy whose father had the same name as that of the actual culprit. It was done at the behest of the landlord to which the real culprit was attached as labourer. The Samiti took up the case of the boy and made attempts for his release. Not only it succeeded in getting the boy released but it also helped him to appear at an examination while in jail".

Thus it appears that a poor is often implicated not due to his involvement but because of his helplessness. The landlords are also in league with the police to torture the innocent poor. It would be further evident from the incident narrated above that the dalits are equally concerned about the provision of education even if it has to be made against odds. We cite another incident to show how the police is biased against the poor people. This also shows that some agency has to be there to help the recurring torture of dalits. The incident is narrated below:

"There is a village named Nathupur in Fatuha. The inhabitants are from different castes. The land, however, belongs in most of the cases to the upper castes. Once an upper caste landlord was done to death. The villagers suspected the hand of a dalit in the murder. Since the man killed happened to be from a rich family, the police acted swiftly to identify the 'culprit'. In this process the man who was suspected to have involvement in the murder was subjected to frequent harassment by the police. The dalits of this village approached the Samiti. After their investigations the workers of the Samiti found the man to be innocent. A senior advocate of Barh, who is associated with the Samiti, went to the police station requesting the officials not to subject the man to unnecessary harassment. The lawyer is so influential and the Samiti is so effective that the police had to relent".

Even the poor toddy-tappers engaged in their traditional occupation are not spared by the police. We cite an instance to illustrate the excesses of police in such matters :

"In the village Khajurar, in Patna district, the Pasis are engaged in their traditional profession of selling toddy. Once a constable approached him for some illegal gratification. In order to avoid unnecessary trouble the Pasi paid a sum of Rs. 500. The trouble did not end here. After this incident he had to supply toddy to the village *Chowkidar* regularly who refused to make any payment for the drink. This matter was brought to the Samiti and at the time of interview, actions were still being contemplated".

The Samiti has also acted as a powerful deterrent against exploitation of the dalits from the anti-social elements. In villages the dalit neighbourhood is an easy prey to all forms of nuisance. The upper castes people select it as safe place for certain activities. Any protest to their advances is violently retaliated. We cite here an instance where the effective intervention of the Samiti helped a dalit who was the victim of such excesses by the caste Hindus.

"There is a village named Ajgara in Barh. It is dominanted by the upper castes. They consume liquor in the neighbourhood inhabited by potters. Once when a potter resisted, he was assaulted and his house was burnt into ashes. The matter was referred to the Samiti which lodged a case with the local police. The culprits were arrested. One of the accused however remains absconding".

The combined strength of the dalits in the Samiti has been successful in ensuring the release of a boy from a dalit family kidnapped for ransom. The incident occurred only recently and is worth narrating :

"The son of one of the scheduled caste families was kidnapped in the village Kharuara by an upper caste criminal. The incident took place in the late night when the boy was returning after attending a marriage ceremony. A ransom of Rs. 1.5 lakh was demanded for his release. The matter was taken by the Samiti which set the administrative machinery into operation. Out of fear, the boy was released immediately without any payment. However, no arrest could be made in this regard".

Earlier bondage had the legitimacy of tradition. Subsequently, it acquired a different dimension. In place of informal bondage we have a situation of debt-slavery. Often such bondage finds sustenance through coercion. The Samiti seems to have been successful in providing redemption to the bonded labourers from the excruciating grip of debt slavery. We cite an example :

> "In village Sahjahan in the district of Patna, a schedule caste peasant took a loan of Rs. 300 to get his daughter married. Subsequently on account of non-payment of loan and the interest thereof the entire family had to pledge itself as bonded labourers working for the money-lender. These persons were denied their wages on refusal to work, they were abused and at times assaulted also. The victims approached the Samiti. A case was instituted against the money-lender. The money-lender wanted to arrive at a compromise with the victims. This was, however, unacceptable to the victims. The matter is pending in the labour court".

It would be evident from the above illustration that the complainant is not subjected to the dictates of the Samiti in seeking redressal to its grievances On his denial for any compromise the Samiti does not act otherwise. We cite another example, were a landlord was forced to free a bonded labourer. The details are narrated below:

> "In village Pandarak a scheduled caste man borrowed some money from an upper caste landlord. As he failed to repay the loan, his son became a bonded labourer attached to the landlord. The son also in a situation of distress took loan from the landlord. One day the boy disappeared from the village. After a few days, he was captured by the landlord somewhere in a town and was brought back to his village. The Samiti took serious note of it and the landlord was forced to release the bonded labourer without payment of the due".

Land is an important source of power in the village. A man without land would be less powerful than a man with land. Land ownership when supported by other sources of income, helps the rich to tighten their hold on the poor who are exploited.

This is evident from an instance where a school teacher belonging to a dominant caste in possession of sufficient land for agriculture is reported to have exploited a dalit to work as bonded labourer. The details are as follows:

> "In Sahjahanpur a scheduled caste man had to borrow a sum of Rs. 300 in the year 1982. Since then he and his family members were working as bonded labourers attached to the landlord. There has been a demand for the repayment of the loan recently. The victim approached the Samiti for help and with the help of the Samiti, made an application to the Labour Inspector claiming a sum of Rs. 1,35,000 (One lakh thirty five thousand) as compensation to the bonded labourer. The matter is still pending, and people are waiting for the decision".

There are instances where the poor people have been found to be the parties in land disputes. Such cases have been amicably settled with the effective intervention of the Samiti. We cite here an instance from Safipur in Khushrupur :

> "There was a dispute between two persons belonging to a scheduled caste. The women work in their families as maid servants in the houses of caste Hindus to enśure safe delivery of children. The two dalits clashed over the possession of a small plot of land allotted to them by the government. The Samiti held a meeting of the dalits in the village to know the truth. After hearing the parties and the witnesses, the land was restored to its legal owner."

The scheduled castes are by and large poor people. Poverty is an unavoidable reality of their life. However, with the availability of education and modern occupational facilities, a few from among them have been able to acquire slightly better position in the economic hierarchy. Such persons have a distinct edge over the rest of the members of their community and are more inclined to associate themselves with identically placed persons from other castes. Such persons exploit their own caste people. They often coerce their own unlucky brethren. These lead to harassment and trouble to those whom they exploit. An instance from Fatuha is cited below:

> "In Parsa one man belonging to one of the scheduled castes has acquired prosperity. He owns land and is in government service. He is more close to the middle range castes than the members of his own caste. He has an instinct to dominate. Once a goat of a poor helpless dalit was intentionally killed by him. The owner of the goat approached the Samiti and requested its legal cell to initiate

a case against the wrongdoer. The Samiti wanted to help the complainant to enter into a compromise. However, on his refusal the legal cell got a case instituted against the culprit. The case is pending in a legal court".

We also have come across an instance where the Samiti had to get itself involved to protect a poor man belonging to one of the intermediate castes from exploitation by a man belonging to one of the scheduled castes and having reputation for violence. We site an instance :

"Chakdaulat is a village in Barh dominated by Kurmis and Dusadhs. There is a pond in that village, which used to be under the control of a man from the Scheduled Caste. This man damaged intentionally the crop of one of the Kurmis while attempting to take water out of the pond. He would not listen to the pleadings of the landowner and threatened him with dire consequences as he was in possession of an illegal arm. The Samiti was brought into action on the request of the landowner. A case has been instituted."

The excesses of a similar nature that involved members of the scheduled castes are narrated to illustrate the illegal advances made by a person having acquired recent prosperity.

Among the scheduled castes the women are the worst sufferers. Since time immemorial they have been subjected to exploitation. They are treated like a commodity by persons belonging to the upper castes. Rape of a dalit female has been an extra-economic way of suppression and exploitation. Earlier the culprit used to be feudal lords. In the present set-up however, the rich among the middle range castes seem to be equally exploitative. We here cite an incident where in spite of the protection promised by the law the parents of a victim of attempted rape refused to institute a case against the culprit :

"There is a village named Kaswa in Bhaktiarpur. A poor man from one of the scheduled castes had to work as a labourer in order to earn his livelihood. He used to work in the fields of a landowner from one of the middle range castes. In fact most of the land in the village belong to these castes. Once while returning from work he saw one of the members of the landed caste entering into his house. He wanted to rape the minor girl of the poor fellow. The girl was crying for help. On hearing the hue and cry persons from neighbourhood gathered around his house and made the culprit leave the house. However, such was the terror of the people of these castes, that in spite of repeated persuasion he refused to institute a case. In fact, he was threatened by the culprit that he would be killed, should he institute a case".

IV

The legal aid programme of the Samiti is operative quite effectively. It is providing succour to people belonging to the poor community in different spheres. As it has been noted earlier, the dalits are subjected to exploitation. They are implicated in false cases. Police tortures them even when they are innocent. The samiti has helped such victims. The Samiti has also been effective in settlement of cases of elementary nature by arranging compromises between the contending parties. This is true, mostly with regard to disputes between relatives or between friends. We cite here an incident involving brothers. The dispute as we would see could be settled amicably with the help of the Samiti. This could be a deterrent to the wastage of meagre resources at the disposal of the quarrelling parties and could also save them from the tortures associated in legal adjudication. The details are cited below:

"In Daniwan the Manjhis are engaged in illegal preparation of liquors. One of the Manjhis encroached upon the land of his own brother. This led to a clash. In the process the man whose land was being encroached was assaulted seriously. The victim lodged a complaint with the police. On the request of the members of the local unit it was decided that the encroached land had to be vacated and compensation had to be paid to the victim. The matter was settled and the complaint was withdrawn".

In a few cases the whole village has been reported to have been involved to find a settlement. We cite here an incident to illustrate the point:

"In village Parsa, in the year 1992 there was a clash between brothers over the possession of land. The parties involved were poor agricultural labourers. When the clash became regular one

> of the brothers approached the caste men of his village. The village unit requested the Samiti. A meeting was called under the auspices of the Samiti. After giving a patient hearing of the parties, the matter was settled".

When the joint family breaks down or when the collateral nuclear members of the families find themselves under strained inter-personal relationship, clashes are frequent and at times violent. Slightest provocation leads to fights if tension is allowed to remain uncontained. There would be immense problem for the contending parties. In such enventualities a quick intervention of the Samiti is highly useful. This would be evident from the incident narrated below :

> "After the death of her husband, Sita Devi of village Bajitpur in Barh was subjected to torture. She was being deprived of her rights to the property left by her husband. Stair-cases were built on her land. The culprit happened to be the brother of her deceased husband. On being approached, the Samiti instructed the trespasser to vacate the land encroached upon and to demolish the illegal structure. This was accepted and the matter ended there."

Thus it appears that in most of the cases the clashes over trifles can be settled easily outside the cumbersome process of legal adjudication. Legal procedures are expensive as well as time-consuming. They also lead to loss of the meagre resources at the disposal of the poor. Absence from workplace to attend the legal courts also amount to loss of wage. In order to avoid such problems and arrive at a mutual settlement Dalits find redressal of grievances with the help of Samiti.

The Samiti has worked to help women in distress. In a situation where a separated wife was deprived of the compensation due to her, she received strong support from the Samiti. We cite the details as follows:

> "In 1977 in village Dariapur, Mudri Devi was married to Mangal Das. In order to help the son-in-law to get a job, the father of the girl paid bribes. On getting the job, the ungrateful son-in-law divorced his wife and married another girl. The matter was referred to the court. The court instructed the husband of the girl to pay a sum of Rs. 500 a month as compensation. In order to deprive the girl of the amount the accused had to pay, he obtained a false

signature of the girl on a document in agreement of for reunion. The matter was taken by the Samiti and it saw to it that the payment of compensation was resumed."

V

The Samiti thus represents an independent innovative institution for redress. It tends to be the initiator of 'action-sets' to ensure delivery of legal services. It has been effective in increasing the access and use of prevalent legal system among dalits. The Samiti seems to have complete faith in the use of law in its fight against exploitation. Legal aid programme of the Samiti is not confined to the provision of counsel at trial stage. In fact its programmes have helped in establishment of an effective fit between the statute book and the deprived. Legal aid provided by the Samiti is 'strategic in nature' because it is oriented to the long run as well as to the immediate advantage or relief and to matters that affect groups rather than isolated individuals. Such measures have enhanced the liberated profile and content of the law itself. Redress of grievances through legal measures has inculcated a sense of efficacy in the provisions of the existing law. Its legal aid personnel are active in different areas playing the role of 'paralegals' or barefoot lawyers. Through its legal awareness programmes the Samiti seems to have increased legal literacy among dalits. Such awareness programmes have heightened sensitivities against injustice among the poor. Its achievements are impressive in spite of the modest budget and simple infrastructure. Where possible, it has helped minimisation of vexatious and avoidable litigation particularly by stinging officials into action for the needed help. The Samiti turns out to be an institution cognate to the indigenous genius through its role in bringing amenable solution to disputes. Dependence upon the important and powerful individuals or dominant castes for settlement of disputes between individuals idenitically placed in the social hierarchy or for settlement of family disputes has been reduced on account of the efforts of the Samiti. Existing resources for redressal of legal rights have been used so effectively that the strategy adopted is perceived to be an innovative solution to an old problem.

REFERENCES

1. Dinesh Khosla, *Myth and Reality of the Protection of Civil Rights Law*, Hindustan Publishing Corporation, Delhi, 1987.
2. Upendra Baxi, 'Legal Assistance to the Poor', in *Economic and Political Weekly*, Vol. 10, No. 27, p. 1005, 1976.
3. R.S Khare, 'Indigenous Culture and Lawer's Law in India' in *Camparative Studies in Society and History*, Vol. 14, 1962, p. 85.
4. Marc Galenter, 'The Abolition of Disabilities — Untouchability and the Law' in the *Untouchables in Contemporary India*, ed. by Michael Mahar, The University of Arizona Press, Tuscon, 1976.
5. R. S. Khare, *op.cit.*
6. *Report of the National Expert Committee on Legal Aid*, 1976.
7. P. D. Mathew, *Babubigha : Scheduled Caste People Show the Way*, Indian Social Institute, New Delhi, 1994.
8. Patricia Gough, "Blinding Justice' in *The Week*, March 3-9, 1995.

5

Encounters and Experiences

Hostility on the part of the embedded and intertia and passivity of the helpless render attempts of the organizations weeded to upliftment of dalits difficult. The workers in the Samiti have narrated in detail their encounters in this regard. These have been documented in order to provide an idea on the problems involved in social work among dalits in the villages.

It is interesting to note that, in spite of long association with the organisation, the social workers encounter problems in the conduct of their duties. The study indicates that there is no clear-cut relation between length of association with the Samiti and propensity to work without experiencing problems. Education also does not appear to be a factor helpful to the social workers in performing their tasks without any difficulty. In fact there is inverse relationship between education and experience of problems. This doesn't mean that educated workers are less capable. In fact in most of the cases they have to shoulder responsibilities that could not be entrusted to persons having sparse education. The difference in the response in this regard may be attributed to the nature of task entrusted to them.

It may also be noted that sex is not an important variable to explain experience of problems in the conduct of work. The females have reported to have encountered more problems than the males. But the difference in this regard is negligible.

It is evident from the responses that the social workers have to work in a very hostile situation. This is because of the fact that the prevalent social structure is intolerable to the rising aspiration of dalits. Dalits have to be docile and passive. They have to accept exploitations as a way of life. Any attempt to resist exploitation leads to violent repression. This is illustrated from the details obtained from the social workers, who, in spite of unfavourable social situation, have been successful in taking the programmes of the Samiti to the grassroots. To quote a social worker:

> "In 1983 the Samiti went to Agwanpur in Barh to initiate the formation of village Samitis. Unfortunately, in the unit that was set up all the crucial positions went to the upper castes. Finding it against the spirit of the Samiti, I helped formation of a Samiti which had dalits as its office-bearers. This was not liked by the upper caste people who had developed a vested interest in the affairs of the Samiti. Once while the meeting of the newly formed village unit was going on, we were surrounded by armed men belonging to upper castes. Out of fear we left that place. It was however with the help of an influential upper caste officer that we could find place in the village after sometimes".

Similar incidents have been reported to have occurred in Gowasha village of Shekhpura. The activities at this place were resisted not only by the upper caste people but also by one of the dominant middle range castes. To quote the social worker :

> "In this village it was decided to have a community hall for the persons of the weaker community having affiliation with the Samiti. This was not liked by the Yadavas of the village. We had to take this matter for legal adjudication. On being declared entitled to the land where the building was to be constructed, the Samiti did not face any resistance from those who earlier did not like the construction".

The main worry of the dominant castes seem to be the possible loss of cheap and unnecessary labour force available to them. To quote a different social worker:

> "In Bhagwanchuk the Samiti decided to unite the Musahars to form units for affiliation to the Samiti. The social worker working for the Samiti were caught hold of by the upper caste people and were told that they would never allow such activities in their village as it might lead to loss of agricultural labour available to them. The little materials that the workers had in their possession were forcibly taken away by these people and they were allowed to leave the village on the request of a dalit of that village who knew them".

Similar incidents have been reported to have taken place at many places. We cite a recent incident in this regard that has been reported from Nawada :

> "A Musahar worker of the Samiti had taken the task of preparing a community pond for the Manjhis. It was not liked by a local contractor whose work suffered on account of large scale desertion of workers from this caste. The contractor, a man from one of the middle range castes and related to a powerful political leader caught hold of a worker and seriously assaulted him. The worker had to be hospitalised. The Samiti took up his case. However, on the request of the above-mentioned political leader, no attempt was made for punishing the culprit".

Attempts to take poor dalits from the clutches of various landed interests have also been resisted. We cite here an incident:

> "In 1991, in a village named Bhelwa Rampur located near Danapur, it was detected that a yound man from a Chamar family had been working as a bonded labourer in the house of an upper caste. It was found that some 20 years back his father had taken some loan from the landlord. To secure loan he had not only mortgaged his land but also pledged himself to work as bonded labour in his house. After the death of this man his son had the same fate. It was however a matter of chance that he could find some papers with regard to the land which his father possessed and was now in illegal possession of the landlord. The people from the Samiti made frequent visits to the village. Once while proceeding to the village, the jeep which was carrying the social workers was surrounded by musclemen of the landlord. In fact the workers had a miraculous escape and had to leave the village".

In village Chirowra (Naubatpur), such is the terror of the dominant castes that it has not been possible for the workers to enter the village to take up the case of the killing of one of its active social workers.

There are instances where the social workers have been implicated in false cases to deter them in their efforts to work among the dalits. We here cite an instance as reported to us by one of the social workers:

> "In Jamalbigha while a camp was in operation, the workers were

falsely implicated in a case involving the theft of cows. The upper caste landlords disturbed the conduct of the activities of the Samiti. Since they failed to substantiate their allegations the social workers were not subjected to further harassment. However, the activities had to be postponed".

On several occasions and at a number of places the non-scheduled castes specially those who exploit dalits have been reported to be intolerant to attempts of the Samiti workers to hold meetings. To quote a respondent:

> "Once in a village named Malti, a health camp was being organised for the scheduled caste population of the village. It was being held on the campus of a primary school. In order to facilitate the accommodation of a large section of beneficiaries, a tent was put on the land in front of the school which belonged to a farmer from one of the middle range castes. The members of this landed caste razed the tent to the ground and continued shouting as long as the programme went on".

Thus it is evident from the above incident that even such activities as have little potentiality to question the exploitation of dalits are not tolerated. The workers of the Samiti have to be patient and calm even in the wake of provocations. Dalits seem to be a commodity in the possession of their masters in the village. They are neither cared nor allowed to be cared.

At times landed interest try to split the dalits. This is done in order to prevent emergence of any unity among them that could be harnessed by the members for attainment of corporate ends for dalits. We here quote a social worker from Nawada:

> "We had the task of forming village units in the villages of Nawada District. In this effort we encountered stiff opposition from landowners of the villages. In one of the villages these people called a meeting of the members of the statutory Panchayat which was dominated by the vested interests. The dalits of the area were "requested" not to co-operate with us. In the light of this development we approached the dalits individually contacting the members of the poor community and were within very short time in a position to form the committee".

In some of the villages the Samiti's members were not allowed to take their vehicles and were deprived of the materials including banners that used to be in their possession. They have been subjected to personal loss on account of their attempts to help dalits in enountering the exploitation by the landed interest. Thus in one case a poor social worker had to bear the loss of crops standing on his small plot of land on account of his efforts to help a scheduled caste person to institute a case against an exploiter who happened to be the member of a middle range caste.

The social workers have also been described as an agents of the Christian missionaries out to convert poor schedule castes to Christianity. This has been reported to have impaired the activities of the Samiti in Saharsa. In a village named Salalpur the workers were described as cheats who had the intention of befooling poor scheduled castes.

In their bid to harass the social workers the landed interests seem to have activated their unholy linkages with the state officials and constabulary. Such linkages are quite common in villages and are an important instrument to help perpetuation of the exploitation of dalits. We here cite an incident that has been reported from a village named Mahuli in Barh. To quote a social worker:

> "In Mahuli we were having a meeting in Chamartoli. The response had been satisfactory. This was not liked by the dominant upper castes of the village. At times such elements felt disturbed on account of the organised resistance of dalits against their exploitation. In order to frustrate the activities of the Samiti, these landed interests implicated me in a false case of dacoity. Since I was arrested in the night, no help could come to me. In the morning however, at the intervention of other social workers the top police official ordered my release".

Similar incident has been reported from Khagaria where the sinster attempts of the poeple in the uniform to harass social workers was frustrated on account of the angry and violent retaliation of a female worker.

> "In Rajajan, Khagaria, some workers had gone to organise the Musahars. These were in a very deplorable condition on account of their poverty, low social status and socio-economic exploitation.

The activities of the workers found encouraging response. This was not liked by the middle range castes who happened to be the dominant caste of the area. Once during the night the workers were detained by the police for having abducted a female. In fact the female happened to be a catholic sister working with other social workers of the Samiti. An attempt was made to explain to the officer the reality of the situation but it appeared that he was acting at the behest of the dominant landed exploiters. The sister got disturbed and was so infuriated that she was about to beat the man in the uniform with her sandle. This worked and we were saved".

This is nothing unusual. In villages the police machinery has its own style of operation. Poor are considered to be thieves and are arrested in spite of their being innocent. It seems that poor cannot be honest and rich cannot be dishonest in the eyes of police. Poverty is the biggest crime capable of leading the poor to trouble. The social workers of the organisation in spite of their being educated have not found exemption from the suspicious eyes of the men in the uniform. We here cite an interesting incident to illustrate this:

> "In 1985 a few social workers had brought seedlings for plantation to promote environmental development under a scheme launched by the Samiti. As they alighted from the train in the night they were caught for being suspect in a theft case about which they had no knowledge. The explanation together with the presence of the seedling in their possession could not facilitate their release. With the help of the Samiti, however, they were released".

There is a greater possibility of being landed in prison in areas where left-oriented activists are in operation. In such areas a dalit has a chance of being suspected as an activist wedded to violence. This has in fact landed some social workers in trouble. We cite here an incident from Jehanabad:

> "In the villages of this district the social workers had gone to help formation of the village units unaware of the fact that the area was tense on account of the killing of the Mukhiya of a Gram Panchayat. One of the social workers was caught on the suspiction of being a Naxalite. He was, however, released at the intervention of the Samiti workers."

On occasions police seem to help the landowners to frustrate the peaceful meetings of dalits organised under the auspices of the Samiti. We cite an incident from Barh:

> "In the year 1992 in the village named Bhadawar a meeting was organised. It was duly permitted by the police officials of the area. However, when the date of the meeting drew close, the permission was cancelled and meeting was not allowed to be held. This was done to facilitate the interest of the landed castes of the area."

In event of a clash between dalits and the landed dominant castes the police invariably supports the latter. This is also because there is dominance of such interests in the police. This would be evident from the incident narrated below:

> "In village Moratalab (Biharsharif) there was a clash between the Chamars and Rajputs over the issue of entry to a temple. The Samiti took this matter to the officials in the police department. The police instead of working in accordance with the spirit of the Constitution sided with the upper castes in keeping the Chamars away from the temple".

The social workers have also to encounter anti-social elements in the village. Such people have the patronage of the politicians and at times they are feared in the local area. They have a tendency to exploit the poor and helpless in the area. People find it difficult to challenge them. While the landed interests and the biased police officals have some reason in frustrating the activities of the organisation, these anti-social elements have their own axe to grind. They have been reported to have created problems through their mischiefs on a number of occasions. We here cite an incident from Hajipur.

> "In village Chamardiha an anti-social element had grabbed 4 acres of land belonging to dalits. The Samiti took up the cause of the exploited and instituted a case against this man. As a result of this, the poor people who owned the land were severely assaulted by this man. On earlier occasions the landed exploiter had threatened the workers of the Samiti on its premises. The injured persons were taken to the local hospital. They were, however, not

provided the attention from the doctors. It was mere chance that the Chief Minister of Bihar who was passing through that way saw the crowd agitating for treatment of the injured. He immediately ordered for the suspension of the doctors. After this incident this land-grabber continued pressure. But there was no let up and ultimately we won the case".

Such undesirable elements have been reported to have made attempts to see that the benefits meant for dalits are diverted to them. The failure on the part of the social workers to comply with such demands had incurred the wrath of such elements. We cite here an incident from Barbigha :

"In 1987, in the village Siday a project was being carried out for providing safe drinking water for the dalits. The upper caste people wanted the installation of the hand pump at their place. In fact it has to be installed in the area occupied by the scheduled castes. The upper caste people threatened the social workers conducting this programme with dire consequences. On finding them unrelenting they caught hold of the social workers and assaulted them physically. Subsequently at the intervention of a sensible and powerful upper caste landlord the matter was settled."

In the institutions that are operative at the block headquarters and where programmes for employment-oriented education are being conducted, the reports of mischief by undesirable elements have been made. To quote an instructor from Fatuha:

"We have a number of job-oriented courses for dalits of the area. This includes training in the skill of type-writing. The students comprise males as well as females. Once an anti-social element entered the training centre. On being challenged he seemed prepared to create futher troubles".

Such elements have been in many of the cases unkind to the female social workers working in the villages. The *Prabhari* (in-charge) of Barh maintained that the female workers have been more than once insulted by persons under the influence of alcohol. We here cite an incident. To quote a social worker :

> "The Samiti has taken up programme for spread of literacy among dalits. Total literacy campaign constituted one such endeavour. Once, while the programme was being conducted in a village named Chero, the female workers who were singing songs to create interest among the dalits were teased. The anti-social elements distrubed the programme by shouting obscenities and calling them prostitutes".

In Bihar there are places where regular illegal payments have to be made to the musclemen of the area in order to carry on even a small business for one's livelihood. Any refusal on the part of the poor invites violent repraisal. Even the rich businessmen are not exempted. In Mokama seems to have become an institutionalised mechanism for extortion. Other places are also having experiences of such exploitation. Even the Samiti workers have to pay money to such elements locally known as *Rangadar* in the villages. We here cite one incident:

> "In the village Dhobichak it was decided to build a community hall for the dalits. The Samiti deputed workers to supervise the construction work. They were also entrusted with the task of purchase of materials for construction. The materials had to be transported in tractors. For each trip of such tractors the workers had to pay a "rangdari tax" of Rs. 200".

The Samiti is operative in many villages of different districts. Dalits are in different stages of mobilisation in the areas where the Samiti is active. In areas where the left extremists are operative, the task to seek support of the dalits for their organisation has been found to be rather difficult. The entry of the Samiti workers are not tolerated by the left extremists who consider such efforts inimical to the mobilisation of the peasantry. They consider it as an attempt to split their constituency. In such areas there is exclusive dominance of particular persuasion. They don't like to work in tandem with even like-minded outfits. Since the Samiti is wedded to peaceful social transformation, its efforts are resisted to the hilt. We cite here a few cases of such encounters in the different villages as reported to us by the social workers.

> "In 1990, in the villages Kharah, Dhanarua and Sultanpur, all

having naxalities the social workers are reported to have been compelled to leave the village. In Sultanpur, they were branded as agents of the Government. However, in Sultanpur the programme of the Samiti could be resumed after a brief lull and continuous dialogue between the workers of the Samiti and the left outfits. In Kălyanpur village under the jurisdiction of Vaishali District the Samiti people were accused of inducting a split in the ranks of the extremists operative in the area. The Samiti was dubbed as the organisation of the capitalists. In this village the execution of the programmes of the Samiti was subjected to immense difficulties. In Jaitia (Fatuha) and in some villages of Punpun the social workers, had frequent encountres with the members of the Indian Peoples Front. However, they were allowed to continue their activities among the dalits as the members of this ultra left party felt convinced about the intentions of the Samiti".

At times the workers of the organisations had to work under constant threat of left organisations. We here cite one instance:

"In Chotka Amaur the workers were holding a meeting of the female unit of the organisation. Their presence was reported to the extremists by the inhabitants of the village. Suddently, the village was surrounded by armed naxalites who made the people flee at the point of gun. The workers tried to convince the naxalites by showing their identity papers. The workers remained surrounded by the naxalites. They slept together and in the morning to the utter surprise of the workers the extremists had left the village".

An incident is reported to have taken place in Barbigha where the social workers were suspected to be the Naxalites. This area happens to be slightly free from the influence of the left extremists. Any unknown person conducting unconventional programmes becomes a suspect in the eyes of landowing castes of the village. We cite here one such incident:

"When we visited Akangardih in Barbigha, we had a new experience. There was a rumour that we are naxalites and had the intention of mobilising the peasantry. While the activities were going on we had to encounter the upper caste people to whom our identity with the Samiti could subsequently convince about our intentions".

There is a proliferation of caste associations among the scheduled castes. Each association is supposed to cater to the needs of its members. Each association has its *Sena*. There have been occasions of encounters such Senas. One incident is cited below: To quote a social worker:

> "We were proceeding to Patna along with members of the Samiti to participate in a meeting. This was not liked by the "dalit sena" operative in the area. The members of the Sena did not want our people to go to Patna. They were forced to be confined at the Khagaria railway station. I was arrested. The police were working at the instruction of the patrons of the dalit Sena. This was resisted by our people who started pelting stones at the police station. To control the mob the police in Khagaria sought additional police force from Saharsa. But the situation had gone out of their control and I had to be released".

6

Evaluation and Suggestions

The Bihar Dalit Vikas Samiti represents a people-oriented radical approach to the problems of dalits. It constitutes a response to help dalits from a situation of crisis demanding immediate intervention. Its basic intent is to organise dalits in search of justice and equality. It is a grassroot movement and operative on behalf of the weak and oppressed. It functions among the depressed sections in the unorganised sector. Its concern for the poor has led it to launch programmes to meet the priority needs of the depressed. The organisation does not claim to have the capacity to bring to an end the enormous problems being encountered by dalits. It also does not claim to have evolved the most appropriate strategy to ameliorate the sad plight of the poor. It however, may claim to have helped dalits to acquire a self-reliant identity. Its policy of preferential treatment for the weaker sections has led to lessening of the disadvantages of caste among its beneficiaries. Awareness building in order to resist exploitation, assertiveness to stake claims due to them with the help of indigenous leadership constitute the important achievements of the organisation. Inculcation of a feeling of self-respect has enabled them to assert for proper treatment. It may not claim to have graduated the dalits from penury to any livable standard or from a situation destitution to state of basic need satisfaction, but it has certainly helped them to elevate themselves from subjecthood to citizenship. The organisation has provided them an opportunity to acquire the needed awareness to stake claims for their due in society. Since it efforts are people-oriented, it has led to articulation and aggregation of people's power. It provides strength to dalits to resist exploitation. It seems to have facilitiated the process of structural change. It has made the dalit conscious and has oriented them to seek social transformation. Its achievements even though modest have impressive consequences in terms of organisational approach to the solution of the problems of the weakest.

The Bihar Dalit Vikas Samiti seeks to acquire a complementary role to help the state in achievement of its commitment for the deprived section of the society. The passive and the inert have been nurtured to become articulate recipients of the inputs percolating from above. It has better rapport with the people than the bureaucrats and development officials have. Organised pressure of the beneficiaries counteracts the disinterestedness of the administration and the opposition of vested interests. The trickle down benefits is susceptible to downward percolation under the pressure from the bottom. Such aggregation of dalits under the auspices of the Samiti operates as a mechanism to correct the hated and derided bureaucracy. Unless persons deprived of the benefits meant for them are organised to bring pressure on administration, it would be difficult to ensure them their due. It has, however, to be noted that its participation in project funded by the state are limited to the amount made available. In fact it does not intend to be mere extension of the state activities.

Its involvement in state sponsored programme is strategic. It seeks to foster people's power to enable dalits to acquire the rights guaranteed in the Constitution. Its intent is to usher in a process of empowering the weak to ensure a process to transform the local situation. Its strategies are in tune with the development model where "the small village group [believe] in mobilising people and organising the poor, generating awareness and putting pressure on the system from below to make it respond to felt needs". In a sense its efforts represent an educative process to prepare the poor to strike at the structural roots of poverty. Such initiatives are needed in a situation characterised by irrelevance of modern state structure as an institution to ensure reallocation of resources on an egalitarian line. In this sense it seems to have an invisible political agenda as its activities have profound political implications. Socially conscious and organised masses, have sharper political articulation. The partial and lopsided input approach to development does not find much favour in the programmes of the organisation. Its ultimate aim seems to make dalits self-reliant by acquiring the needed political resources. The Samiti has gone beyond the charity orientation characterising the orientation of voluntary organisations in the past.[1]

The Bihar Dalit Vikas Samiti represents an unique experiment to provide immediate support to dalits to secure justice. It is a mechanism to arrange for the redressal of discrimination of the helplessness by seeking proper implementation of the provisions of law. Such impressive have been its achievements in this regard that atrocities on dalits in the areas of its operation are on wane. The dalits are no longer unsafe in these areas. It has also been successful in raising people's consciousness through intensive education. Its programmes have helped in development of human resources. Since social workers work among dalits the organisation has been successful in helping them have a better appreciation of their own conditions. It has helped itself to build grassroot support for and trust in the organisation.

It is non-violent and orderly in its struggle against injustice. While creating a new space for dalits in the society it has not to be found entrapped in unnecessary and avoidable confrontation with the state or the political parties. Opposition to exploitative power structure at the grassroot and occasional conflict with corrupt officials at times lead the Samaiti to adopt a confrontational approach. In other situation it seeks to extend its activities nurturing as non-confrontational orientation among its workers. It has conflictive approach to situation of discrimination and exploitation and has reconciliatory approach as if support implementation of state-sponsored programmes for dalits. In a few areas it has found support among the clients associated with the left movement. It, however, does not seem inclined to coalesce with other movements having identical priorities but different approaches. Affiliation with organisations having identical concern has also not been tried at. Outside ideological linkages are not encouraged. Its activities seem to be oriented not towards accentuating social contradictions and class conflict. However, it intends to foster class collaboration. In a broad sense it belongs to the large section of such voluntary organisations that have the objective of "pursuing an independent and local pro-people role cooperating with appropriate and fighting against it when necessary".[2]

The concern for the poor and programmes to help dalits to enable them to meet their priority needs constitute the important components of the programme. The Samiti is, however, not confined to these 'passive variables' of development. Its ultimate goal is to ensure people's participation fundamental to a genuine process of development. In this respect its achievements have been impressive. It has helped in institutionalisation of collective action of dalits. It has helped them to assert. Initiated as an outsider's programme it has adopted strategies to foster leadership qualities among its clients. It has recruited all its executive and administrative staff from its membership of poor and exploited. It has also ensured career to dalits in an organisation for their own uplift. This has ensured spread of its activities. Flexibility, open-endedness experimentation and examination characterise its strategies. Its founder is the primemover whose powerful network and its impressive activation has enforced credibility in the efficacy of the organisation. Its repect for local perspective has led it to orient its programmes to suit the local needs and aspirations. It has the capacity to understand local needs, problems and resources and has also been successful in involving local people's participation. It has helped in preparing people for participation and has helped emergence of decentralised leadership among dalits. Between the social workers the pattern of communication is by and large lateral. Consultation rather than command characterises the dominant pattern of interaction between the constituents. It differs significantly from the hierarchic command system. It has greater proximation with organic rather that mechanistic style of functioning. It also represents a simple professional and managerial enterprise to implement programmes for the benefit of dalits. People's involvements at the decision-making level has been quite marked. The dalit workers might not have learnt the skill of running an organisation and might not have interacted with bureaucrats and top leaders in absence of this organisatio

Horizontal alignment in order to be sustainable has to ensure fulfilment to the priority needs of the people. There are in every organisation a few otherwise inclined workers that tend to remain indifferent routine workers. The Samiti is not an exception. It has in its fold at least a few workers interested in their own survival without doing much work. Such activists in turn tend to be indifferently inclined to the work of the Samiti. Inertia of the locally positioned leadership at times leads to neglect and insensitivity. Lack of proper educational qualification and needed professional training poses a big challenge to the sustenance of the arrangement being sought to be enforced. Its expansion has led to emergence of bureaucratic inclination among its workers. There is a transparent urge on the part of workers to get themselves more to official work than to fieldwork. This is dangerous. The leadership is in fact seem to alive to this affliction. Its attempt to empower the elected leadership at the grassroot to ensure proper supervision over the workers is an attempt in that direction. Professionalism wedded to social uplift through dedicated endeavours have to be accorded more emphasis. It seems paradoxical that payment for sustenance instead of ensuring dedication has led the workers to think that there involvement in this movement is that of an employee. It seems that in order to avoid such development an attempt to reorient the strategy for recruitment of workers have to be tried. Payments for sustenance should be performance-oriented. Career-orientation reminiscent of bureaucratic work culture may spoil the dreams of its founder leader. Wages may be increased but not to make it an institution to suite the career of its workers.

The Samiti is opposed to shift its activities to suite the frequent fluctuations in the state sponsored schemes. The 'strings' of foreign fund and benevolence of states' paltry assistance same of its programmer does not have twisted the priorities of the organisation. Even the programmes characterised by dependence on outside money have inherent limitation as flow of funds may not be a permanent feature. There is a need to initiate income generating programmes by the Samiti to strengthen its own resource base and to suite the economic meeds of the poor. Socially vulnerables are more subjected to exploitation in a situation of economic distress. In absence of such programmes tensions between the immediate aspirations of the masses and the deferred orientation of the organisation may assume an unmanageable dimension.

Thus the Samiti is not an idle populist organisation wedded to rhetoric. It is an action-oriented institution. Such experiments have to be replicated elsewhere. Its lessons provide valuable clues to evolve effective strategies to ensure participation and justice. Such experiments indicate that, in spite of inherent limitations and structural inequality, it is possible to help the distressed in their struggle against exploitation. Such action groups are poised to "create new spaces" in civil society so that conscious people involved in thousands of micro-struggle can come to some kind of macro-perspective which nourishes the well-being of the community. Its achievements would help considerably in identification of effective strategies for achievements of goals that remain unattained in the present circumstances. Success of such initiative would contribute towards emergence of viable organisations of the depressed sections of the society.

REFERENCES

1. Bunker Roy, 'Voluntary Agencies and Government: The Indian Experience' in *Images of Rural India in the Twentieth Century*, ed. by Alok Bhatia and Peter Bumka, Sterling Publishers Pvt Ltd., New Delhi, 1992, p. 91.
2. S.R. Pandey, *Community Action for Social Justice*, Sage Publications, 1991, p. 235.

APPENDICES

APPENDIX I

Organisational Rules and Operational Infrastructure

The Bihar Dalit Vikas Samiti was not envisaged as a bureaucratic institution but as a people's movement. We slowly realised, however, that even a movement needs operational infrastructures and a minimum of organisational rules. This is more so when it moves from small group interests to regional or national level concerns or takes up programmes involving finances. With many trials and errors, we have developed a double-layer system of organisation and monitoring—one from above and the other from below. (See Table I-1).

The General Body above consists of the founding members of the Samiti and others who are invited. It is the ultimate decision making body of the Samiti.

The Governing Body generally consists of nine members appointed by the General Body. They hold office for one year but can be re-elected. The Governing Body has all the powers delegated to it by the General Body.

The Director is appointed by the Governing Body and is overall in charge.

The Prabhari is the regional in charge. There are eighteen regions today with 100 to 200 units under them.

Each region has a Regional Managing Committee consisting of the *Prabhari* (Chairman), another volunteer elected from among the volunteers of the region, two *Pramukhs* and a well-wisher from outside. The Managing Committee appointed by the Director, functions for one year, but the members can be re-elected. The functioning of the Regional Managing Committee is still in the experimental stage.

Volunteers are part-time or full time collaborators who carry on the work of the Samiti.

The organisational structure from the General Body to the *Prabhari* and volunteers reminds one of a bureaucratic set up. However, nearly all the members at different levels except two or three in the Governing Body are from the Dalit community. They are not paid officers but honorary members committed to serve the community. Moreover, this organisational set up is balanced by another infrastructure from below.

Table 1

BDVS Organisational Set up

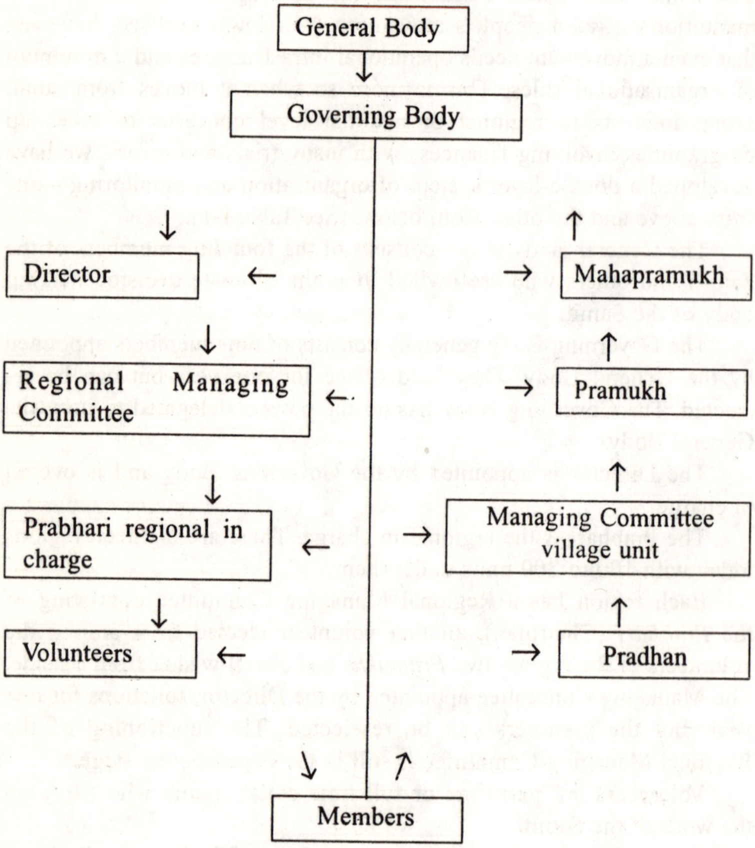

At the first stage from below we have the members of a village unit. Any ten or more Dalit families can come together and form a village unit by contributing Rs. 5 to the village unit. Every 10 members of a unit, spontaneously grouped among themselves from a sub-unit and elect a *Pradhan* (sub-unit leader) from among themselves. All the *Pradhans* of a village unit together elect the village unit managing Committee from among themselves or if the number of Pradhans is small, from all the members of the village unit. The Managing Committee will consist of a President, Secretary, Treasurer and at least two advisers. The Committee meets at least once a month.

The village unit can apply for affiliation to the Bihar Dalit Vikas Samiti as associate members by submitting the required documents and a contribution of Rs. 100.

The Presidents and secretaries of 15 village units elect a *Pramukh* (area leader) from among themselves. If there are five or more area leaders in a region, the *Pramukhs* elect a *Mahapramukh* (regional leader) from among themselves.

Every region will have an Advisory Committee consisting of the *Prabhari,* another volunteer elected from the volunteer of the region, the *Mahapramukh* and another *Pramukh* nominated by the *Prabhari* and a local well-wished of the Samiti nominated by the *Prabhari* and appointed by the Director. The Advisory Committee will hold the position for one year. The *Mahapramukh* will attend the Governing Body meeting if it is held in his region. All these positions are honorary.

The *Pramukhs* and *Mahapramukhs* will keep in touch with the *Prabhari* and as far as possible, coordinate the activities of the respective regions. *Prabhari* will call their meetings at least once in three months.

The Presidents and Secretaries and other *Pradhans* of each unit under a *Pramukh* will work together with the volunteers and the *Prabhari* for the activities of their respective areas. Expenses for meetings, travel etc. will be met by voluntary contributions from local units and donations received from other sources.

The above organisational and mobilisation-based infrastructure was developed through the experience and trial of many years. We are still facing some problems.

1. All the units or all the members do not have the same level of commitment.

2. Most of the work involve unpaid and voluntary service and hence dependent on the initiative or interest of individuals.
3. Most of the activities involve finance. Since nearly all the people are landless agricultural labourers, this becomes a problem.
4. There is a lot of paper work involved which requires time, energy and finance.

We feel that all these problems can be solved to some extent by recruiting the right candidates and by giving them proper training. There are many young people who can be motivated to serve their communities. Perhaps, a most important aspect in this connection is the need for well planned economic programmes for the village units in order to make them self-reliant.

APPENDIX - II

DISTRIBUTION OF SOCIAL WORKERS AMONG DALITS IN THE VILLAGES

TABLE II-1 : Sexwise Distribuction of Social Workers

Place	Male		Female	
	No.	%	No.	%
Barh	17	80.9	04	10.0
Barbigha	06	66.6	03	33.3
Biharsharif	07	100.0		
Dhanarua	05	71.4	02	28.5
Fatuha	09	75.0	03	25.0
Hajipur	06	75.0	02	25.0
Jahanabad	06	100.0	—	—
Khagaria	06	100.0	—	—
Nawada	04	80.0	01	20.0
New Delhi	04	100.0	—	—
Patna	08	100.0	—	—
Raghopur	04	80.0	01	20.0
Saharsa	04	100.0	—	—
Samastipur	03	60.0	02	40.0
Total		83.17		16.82

TABLE II-2 : Placement of Female Workers

Place	Female	Percentage
Barh	0.4	22.2
Barbigha	0.2	16.6
Biharsharif	—	—
Dhanarua	0.2	11.1
Fatuha	0.3	16.6
Hajipur	02	11.1
Jahanabad	—	—
Khagaria	—	—
Nawada	0.1	5.5
New Delhi	—	—
Patna	—	—
Raghopur	0.1	5.5
Saharsa	—	—
Samastipur	0.2	11.1
Total	16.82	13.00

TABLE II-3 : Agewise Distribution of Social Workers

Place	Below 20	21-30	31-40	41-50	51+
Barh	—	52.3	28.5	19.0	—
Barbigha	—	55.5	33.3	11.1	
Biharsharif	—	42.8	57.1	—	—
Dhanarua	14.2	42.8	42.8	—	—
Fatuha	16.6	25.0	41.6	16.6	-
Hajipur	—	62.5	12.5	12.5	12.5
Jahanabad	50.0	33.3	16.6	—	
Khagaria	16.6	50.0	33.3	—	
Nawada	—	60.0	20.0	20.0	—
New Delhi	75.0	25.0	—	—	—
Patna	—	62.5	37.5		
Raghopur	80.0	20.0	—	—	
Saharsa	—	25.0	50.0	25.0	—
Samastipur	—	40.0	60.0	—	—
Total	2.80	48.59	35.51	11.12	1.87

TABLE II-4 Religionwise Distribution of Social Workers

Place	Hindu	Muslim	Christian
Barh	61.1	4.71	33.3
Barbigha	66.6	—	33.3
Biharsharif	71.4	14.21	14.2
Dhanarua	28.5	—	71.4
Fatuha	66.6	—	33.3
Hajipur	75.6	—	25.2
Jahanabad	50.3	—	53.0
Khagaria	16.61	—	83.3
Nawada	80.4	—	20.0
New Delhi	75.3	—	25.1
Patna	100.0	—	—
Raghopur	60.3	—	40.2
Saharsa	50.2	—	50.2
Samastripur	100.0	—	—
Total	69.4	1.82	36.6

TABLE II-5 : Caste among the Social Workers

Place	Chamar	Dusadi	Pasi	Manjhi	Mali	Kurmi	Teli	Koeri	Tanti	Carpenter		Shaikh	Shai	Kayastha	Santhal
Barh	10	03	01	01	01	01	01	01	01	01		—	—	—	—
	16.9	13.6	20.0	25.0	23.3	100.0	100.0	100.0	50.0	50.0					
Barbigha	05	04													
	8.4	18.1													
Biharsharif	06														
	10.1														
Dhanarua	04	02													
	6.7	9.0													
Fatuha	04	03	01	—	01	01	01	01							
	6.7	13.6	20	100.0	33.3	50.0	50.0								
Hajipur	06	01	01												
	10.1	4.5	20.0												
Jehanabad	05	01													
	8.4	4.5													
Khagaria	06														
	10.1														
Nawada	02	01	01	01											
	3.3	4.5	20.0	25.0											
New Delhi	04														
	6.7														
Patna	02	03	01	—	—	01	01								
	3.3	13.6	20.0	—	—	33.3	50.0								
Raghopur	01	01	—	01	01										
	1.6	4.5	—	25.0	50.0										
Saharsa	02	01	—	01											
	3.3	4.5	—	25.0											
Samastipur	02	02													
	3.3	9.0													
Total	59	22	05	04	01	03	—	—	01	01	01	02	02	01	01
	55.1	20.5	4.6	3.7	0.9	2.0	0.93	0.93	0.93	1.87	1.87	0.93	0.93		

TABLE II-6 : Payment of Stipend to Social Workers

Place	Below 200	200-400	401-600	601-800	801 1000	1001-1200	1201 and above
Barh			01	01	03	07	09
			11.1	8.3	7.8	35.0	32.1
Barbigha			01	01	03	02	02
			11.1	8.3	7.8	10.0	7.1
Biharsharif			03	01	—	01	02
			33.3	8.3	—	5.0	7.1
Dhanaura			—	01	04	01	01
				8.3	10.5	5.0	3.5
Fatuha			01	—	04	05	02
			11.1	—	10.5	25.0	7.1
Hajipur			02	01	03	—	02
			22.2	8.3	7.8	—	7.1
Jehanabad			—	02	04	—	—
				16.6	10.5	—	—
Khagaria			—	—	03	01	02
					7.8	5.0	7.1
Nawada			—	02	02	—	01
				16.6	5.2	—	3.5
New Delhi							04
							14.2
Patna					02	06	
					16.6	15.7	
Raghopur			01	01	03		
			11.1	8.3	7.8		
Saharsa			—	—	—	02	02
						10.0	7.1
Samastipur			—	—	03	01	01
					7.8	5.0	3.5
Total			09	12	38	20	28
			8.4	11.2	35.5	18.6	26.1

TABLE II-7 : Length of Association with the Samiti

Place	1 Year	2 Years	3 Years	4 Years	5 Years	6 Years	7 Years	8 Years	9 Years	10 Years	11 Years
Barh	01	—	—	03	01	06	04	01	03	01	01
	9.0	—	—	33.3	6.2	33.3	40.0	25.0	60.0	16.6	25.0
Barbigha	02	01	01	—	03	—	—	01	01	—	—
	18.1	9.0	8.3	—	18.7	—	—	25.0	100.0	—	—
Biharsharif	03	01	01	—	01	01	—	—	—	—	
	27.2	—	8.3	11.1	—	5.5	10.0				
Dhanarua	—	02	02	01	—	—	01	—	—	01	—
	18.1	16.6	11.1	10.0	16.6						
Fatuha	02	03	01	01	01	02	01	—	01		
	18.1	8.3	11.1	12.5	33.3						
Jehanabad	01	—	01	01	01	01	01				
	9.0	—	8.3	11.1	6.2	5.5	10.0				
Khagaria	—	—	—	—	01	01	01	01			
	6.2	5.5	10.0	25.0							
Nawada	01	01	—	—	02	—	—	01			
	9.0	9.0	—	—	12.5	25					
New Delhi	01	—	01	01							
	9.0	—	8.3	11.1							
Patna	—	01	01	—	03	03					
	9.0	8.3	—	18.7	16.6						
Raghopur	—	01	02	—	01	01					
	9.0	16.6	—	6.2	5.5						
Saharsa	—	—	—	—	—	02	01	01			
	11.1	10.0	16.6								
Samastipur	—	—	01	—	01	01	01	01			
	8.3	6.2	5.5	20.0	16.67						

TABLE II-8 : Frequency of Spatial Mobility

Place	Worked at one place	Worked at two place	Worked at three place	Worked at four place	Worked at five place	Worked at six place
Barh	07	07	07	—	—	—
	25.9	19.4	25.9	—	—	—
Barbigha	03	03	01	02	—	—
	11.1	8.3	3.7	16.6	—	—
Biharsharif	04	01	01	—	01	—
	14.8	2.7	3.7	—	25.0	—
Dhanarua	01	03	02	01	—	—
	3.7	8.3	7.4	8.3	—	—
Fatuha	03	05	01	02	—	01
	11.1	13.8	3.7	16.6	—	100.0
Hajipur	02	01	03	01	01	—
	7.4	2.7	11.1	8.3	25.0	—
Jehanabad	01	01	02	01	01	—
	3.7	2.7	7.4	8.3	25.0	—
Khagaria	—	02	02	02	—	—
	5.5	7.4	7.4	—	—	—
Nawada	01	02	01	01	—	—
	3.7	5.5	3.7	8.3	—	—
New Delhi	03	01	—	—	—	—
	11.1	2.7	—	—	—	—
Patna	01	04	03	—	—	—
	3.7	11.1	11.1	—	—	—
Raghopur	01	03	01	—	—	—
	3.7	8.3	3.7	—	—	—
Saharsa	—	01	01	02	—	—
	2.7	3.7	16.6	—	—	—
Samastipur	—	02	02	—	05	—
	5.5	7.4	—	25.0	—	—
Total	27	36	27	12	04	01
	25.23	33.64	25.23	11.21	3.74	0.93

TABLE II-9 : Change in Assignments

Place	No	Once	Twice	Thrice	More than thrice
Barh	12	02	03	04	—
	24.4	8.0	20.0	30.7	—
Barbigha	06	01	02	—	—
	12.2	4.0	13.3	—	—
Biharsharif	04	—	02	01	—
	8.1	—	13.3	7.6	—
Dhanarua	02	03	01	—	01
	4.0	12.0	6.6	—	20.0
Fatuha	07	03	01	—	01
	14.2	12.0	6.6	—	20.0
Hajipur	03	04	—	01	—
	6.1	16.0	—	7.6	—
Jehanabad	02	02	01	01	—
	4.0	8.0	6.6	7.6	—
Kagaria	—	02	—	03	01
	—	8.0	—	23.0	20.0
Nawada	02	01	—	02	—
	4.0	4.0	—	15.3	—
New Delhi	03	—	—	01	—
	6.1	—	—	7.6	—
Patna	03	04	01	—	—
	6.1	16.0	6.6	—	—
Raghopur	03	02	—	—	—
	6.1	8.0	—	—	—
Saharsa	—	—	03	—	01
	—	—	20.0	20.0	—
Samastipur	02	01	01	—	01
	4.0	4.0	6.6	—	20.0
Total	49	25	15	13	05
	45.7	23.3	14.0	12.1	4.6

TABLE II-10 : Reaction to Payment Received

Place	Satisfied		Dissatisfied	
	No.	%	No.	%
Barh	—	—	21	20.1
Barbigha	01	33.3	08	7.6
Biharsharif	—	—	07	6.7
Dhanarua	—	—	07	6.7
Fatuha	01	33.3	11	10.5
Hajipur	—	—	08	7.6
Jehanabad	—	—	06	5.7
Khagaria	—	—	06	5.7
Nawada	—	—	05	4.8
New Delhi	-8	—	04	3.8
Patna	—	—	08	7.6
Raghopur	01	33.3	04	3.8
Saharsa	—	—	04	3.8
Samastipur	—	—	05	4.8
Total	03	2.8	104	97.2

TABLE II-11 : Willingness to work on the Same Stipend

Place	Yes		No	
	No.	%	No.	%
Barh	11	25.0	10	15.8
Barbigha	05	11.3	04	6.3
Biharsharif	02	4.5	05	7.9
Dhanarua	—	—	07	11.1
Fatuha	07	15.9	05	7.9
Hajipur	06	13.6	02	3.1
Jehanabad	02	4.5	04	6.3
Khagaria	01	2.2	05	7.9
Nawada	02	4.5	03	4.7
New Delhi	—	—	04	6.3
Patna	04	9.0	04	6.3
Raghopur	02	2.5	03	4.7
Saharsa	01	2.2	04	6.3
Samastipur	01	2.2	04	6.3
Total	44	41.1	63	58.8

TABLE II-12 : Problems in Discharge of Duties

Place	Yes		No	
	No	%	No	%
Barh	13	16.2	08	30.7
Barbigha	08	10.0	01	3.8
Biharsharif	07	8.7	—	—
Dhanarua	06	7.5	01	3.8
Fatuha	10	12.5	01	3.8
Hajipur	04	5.0	04	15.3
Jehanabad	06	7.5	—	—
Khagaria	06	7.5	—	
Nawada	04	5.0	01	3.8
New Delhi	03	3.7	01	3.8
Patna	02	2.5	06	23.0
Raghopur	02	2.5	03	11.5
Saharsa	04	5.0	—	—
Samastipur	05	6.2	—	
Total	80	74.7	26	24.3

TABLE II-13 : Recruitment of Social Workers

Place	Relatives	Own initiative	Workers in the organization
Barh	03 30.0	08 28.5	10 15.1
Barbigha	03 30.0	02 7.1	04 6.0
Biharsharif	— 14.2	04 4.5	03 —
Dhanarua	02 20.0	01 3.5	04 6.0
Fatuah	01 10.0	02 7.1	07 10.6
Hajipur	01 10.0	03 10.7	04 6.0
Jehanabad	— 3.5	02 7.5	04 —
Khagaria	— 3.5	01 7.5	05 —
Nawada	— —	— 6.0	04 —
New Delhi	01 3.5	03 4.5	— —
Patna	— 7.1	02 9.0	06
Raghopur	— 01	— 7.5	05 —
Saharsa	— 6.0	04 3.7	04 —
Samastipur	02 7.1	03 4.5	— —
Total	10 9.3	28 26.1	66 61.6

TABLE II-14 : Kins as Social Workers

(Percentages)

Place	None	Brother or sister	Father or Mother %	Cousin	Other distant relations
Barh	13 20.0	— —	02 100.0	06 60.0	— —
Barbigha	05 7.6	01 14.2	— —	— —	02 11.7
Biharsharif	05 7.6	01 14.2	— —	— —	01 5.8
Dhanarua	01 1.5	— 20.0	— 11.7	02 —	02 —
Fatuha	06 9.2	01 14.2	— —	01 10.0	02 11.7
Hajipur	06 9.2	01 14.2	— —	— —	01 5.8
Jehanabad	04 6.1	— —	— —	01 10.0	01 5.8
Khagaria	05 7.6	01 14.2	— —	— —	— —
Nawada	01 1.5	— —	— 23.5	— —	04 —
New Delhi	03 4.5	— —	— —	— —	— —
Patna	08 12.3	— —	— —	— —	— —
Raghopur	02 3.0	02 28.5	— —	— —	01 5.8
Saharsa	01 1.5	— —	— —	— —	03 17.6
Samastipur	05 7.6	— —	— —	— —	— —
Total	65 60.7	07 6.5	02 1.8	10 9.3	17

TABLE II-15 : Compositional Forms of the Family

Place	Sub-nuclear	Nuclear	Supplemented nuclear	Collateral joint	Lineal collateral joint		Joint
Barh	05	06	02	—	04	02	02
	71.4	21.4	15.3	—	17.3	7.6	28.5
Barbigha	—	02	01	01	04	01	—
	—	7.1	7.6	3.3	17.3	3.8	—
Biharsharif	—	03	—	—	03	01	—
	10.7	—	—	13.0	3.8	—	—
Dhanarua	—	01	—	—	01	04	01
	—	3.5	—	—	4.3	15.3	14.2
Fatuha	01	04	01	01	01	03	01
	14.2	14.2	7.6	33.3	4.3	11.5	14.2
Hajipur	—	02	01	—	02	02	01
	—	-7.1	7.6	—	8.7	7.6	24.2
Jehanabad	—	01	01	01	—	03	—
	—	3.5	7.6	33.3	—	11.5	—
Khagaria	—	01	01	—	—	03	01
	—	3.5	7.6	—	—	11.5	14.2
Nawada	01	01	01	—	01	—	01
	14.2	3.5	7.6	—	4.3	—	14.2
New Delhi	—	02	02	—	—	—	—
	7.1	15.3	—	—	—	—	—
Patna	—	01	02	—	04	01	—
	—	3.5	15.3	—	17.3	3.8	—
Raghopur	—	01	01	—	01	02	—
	—	3.5	7.6	—	4.3	7.6	—
Saharsa	—	01	—	—	01	02	—
	—	3.5	—	—	4.3	7.6	—
Samastipur	—	02	—	—	01	02	—
	—	7.1	—	—	4.3	7.6	—
Total	07	28	13	03	23	26	07
	6.5	26.1	12.1	2.8	21.5	24.3	6.5

APPENDIX - III

TABLE III-1 : Details of Men's Units as on 30-09-95

	As on 31-3-95		From April-Sept		Total as on 30.9.95	
	Units	Members	Units	Members	Units	Members
Barbigha	180	5085	13	340	193	5425
Barh	205	6125	12	247	217	6372
Biharsharif	60	1371	7	135	67	1506
Dhanarua	91	2726	10	285	101	3011
Fatuha	104	2840	24	364	128	3204
Hajipur	60	1258	5	222	65	1480
Jahanabad	119	3872	14	257	133	4129
Jhajha	79	1965	6	109	85	2074
Khagaria	78	3004	7	272	85	3276
Kharagpur	18	250	13	191	31	441
Mokama	36	995	18	249	54	1244
Muzaffarpur	51	1686	5	159	56	1845
Nawada	75	1838	23	748	98	2586
Patna	47	906	18	279	65	1185
Raghopur	72	2407	9	222	81	2629
Saharsha	66	2062	4	90	70	2152
Samastipur	74	1408	10	155	84	1563
	1415	39798	198	4324	1613	44122
% increase					13.99	10.86

TABLE III-2 : Details of woMen's Units as on 30-09-95

	As on 31-3-95		From April-Sept		Total as on 30.9.95	
	Units	Members	Units	Members	Units	Members
Barbigha	44	902	4	71	48	973
Barh	88	1942	6	109	94	2051
Biharsharif	7	127	9	146	16	272
Dhanarua	8	189	3	71	11	260
Fatuha	41	819	17	225	58	1044
Hajipur	26	389	6	87	32	476
Jahanabad	19	543	2	51	21	594
Jhajha	13	232	2	42	15	274
Khagaria	41	1109	5	84	46	1193
Kharagpur	36	450	23	322	59	772
Mokama	20	338	12	214	32	602
Muzaffarpur	19	480	5	77	24	557
Nawada	30	627	7	131	37	758
Patna	13	338	7	143	20	481
Raghopur	52	1107	30	453	82	1560
Saharsha	9	257	6	97	15	354
Samastipur	66	1311	3	46	69	1357
	532	11209	147	2369	679	13578
% increase					27.63	21.13

TABLE III-3 : Membership Growth 01.4.95 to 30.9.95

	Men's Member		Women's Member		Total Units	Total Member Families
	Unit	Families	Units	Families		
As on March 31, 95	1,415	39,798	532	11,209	1,947	51,007
As on Sept. 30, 95	1,613	44,122	679	13,578	2,292	57,700
Percentage Increase during Six months	13.99	10.86	27.63	21.13	17.00	13.00
Percentage Increase during 1994-95	20.6	14.7	45.2	37.4	26.4	19.0

TABLE III-4 : Progress of Societies (Men)
(01.04.95 to 30.09.95)

Name of Region	Number of units as on 31.03.95	Amount deposited as on 31.03.95	Number of men units during April-Sept.	Amount deposited	Total number of units as on 30.09.95	Total amount deposited as on 30.9.95
Barbigha	65	16,335.00	13	2,888.50	78	19,223.50
Barh	124	46,561.00	18	12,238.00	142	58,799.00
Biharsharif	22	5,876.00	10	2,175.00	32	8,051.00
Dhanarua	19	6,488.00	26	2,376.00	45	8,864.00
Fatuha	50	11,271.00	25	5,790.00	75	17,061.00
Hajipur	26	9,805.00	9	4,295.00	35	14,100.00
Jahanabad	9	1,600.00	19	3,040.00	28	4,640.00
Jhajha	40	8,768.00	11	3,565.00	51	12,333.00
Khagaria	55	24,470.00	9	4,371.00	64	28,841.00
Kharagpur	12	15,450.00	5	8,495.00	17	23,945.00
Mokama	33	6,571.50	16	7,845.00	49	14,416.50
Muzaffarpur	8	1,650.00	2	3,325.00	10	4,975.00
Nawada	14	4,288.00	28	1,700.00	42	5,988.00
Patna	26	5,885.00	15	3,916.00	41	9,801.00
Raghopur	18	5,953.75	9	1,146.00	27	7,099.75
Saharsha	12	4,374.00	12	3,090.00	24	7,464.00
Samastipur	36	9,636.00	7	6,804.50	43	16,440.50
	569	1,84,982.25	234	77,060.00	803	2,62,042.25
% increase					41.12	41.65

TABLE III-5 : Progress of Societies (women)
(01.04.95 to 30.09.95)

Name of Region	Number of units as on 31.03.95	Amount deposited as on 31.03.95	Number of men units during April-Sept.	Amount depo-sited	Total number of units as on 30.09.95	Total amount depo-sited as on 30.9.95
Barbigha	31	16,662.00	4	4,744.00	35	21,406.00
Barh	73	49,549.00	8	11,799.00	81	61,348.00
Biharsharif	4	1,701.00	4	1,093.00	8	2,794.00
Dhanarua	5	2,220.00	2	562.00	7	2,782.00
Fatuha	39	9,770.00	23	10,910.00	62	20,680.00
Hajipur	26	16,783.00	6	4,700.00	32	21,483.00
Jahanabad	5	485.00	13	1,470.00	18	1,955.00
Jhajha	7	2,845.00	2	2,340	9	5,185
Khagaria	29	16,613.00	4	2,035.00	33	18,648.00
Kharagpur	29	25,600.00	18	18,565.00	47	44,165.00
Mokama	17	16,915.00	11	8,270.00	28	25,185.00
Muzaffarpur	17	6,567.00	10	18,055.00	27	24,622.00
Nawada	15	5,121.00	11	1,110.00	26	6,231.00
Patna	14	2,650.00	7	4,535.00	21	7,185.00
Raghopur	39	35,394.50	91	39,535.00	130	74,929.50
Saharsha	2	150.00	5	680.00	7	830.00
Samastipur	37	29,364.50	6	11,164.00	43	40,528.50
	389	2,38,390.00	225	1,41,567.00	614	3,79,957.00
% increase					57.84	59.38

TABLE III-6 : Growth Pattern of Societies

	Men's Unit	Contribution in Rs.	Women's Units	Contribution in Rs.	Total Units	Total Contribution in Rs.
As on March 31, 95	569	1,84,982.25	389	2,38,390.00	958	4,23,372.25
As on 30 Sept. 95	803	2,62,042.25	614	3,79,957.00	1,417	6,41,999.25
Percentage Increase during Six months	41.12	41.65	47,84	59.38	47	51.63
Percentage Increase during 1994-95	57.0	61.9	81.0	97.3	66.3	80.0

TABLE III-7 : The Number of Trainees at the Employment Oriented Training Centres

Name of Region	Electronics	Typing	Tailoring	Embroidery
Barbigha		85	25	
Barh	42	144	27	
Biharsharif		50		
Dhanarua		53	42	
Fatuha		146	34	22
Hajipur		86	15	
Jahanabad		112	70	30
Jhajha	30	88		
Khagaria	29	101		
Kharagpur				
Mokama		29		
Muzaffarpur	25		25	
Nawada		47		
Patna	43	125	44	11
Raghopur				
Saharsha		20		
Samastipur				
	169	1086	282	63

Notes :

Total Number of Students enrolled in the Six Monthly Courses : 1600

Total Expected During the year : 3200

Total Trained during 1994-1995 : 2586

INDEX